Dear Code Breaker

**The letters of Margaret Rock
(Bletchley Park Code Breaker)
&
John Rock
(Parachute and Glider Forces Pioneer)**

Kerry Howard

First published in Great Britain 2013
BookTower Publishing
Redditch, Worcestershire

www.booktowerpublishing.co.uk
www.bletchleyparkresearch.co.uk

ISBN 978-09557164-5-4
BookTower Publishing

A CIP catalogue record for this book is available from the British
Library.

Set in Georgia
Printed and Bound by CreateSpace

Contents

ACKNOWLEDGMENTS

This book and accompanying website exists because of the generosity of Charles and Jane Foster, who enthusiastically let me into their lives and gave me free reign over Margaret's papers. A few words of thanks here does not do justice to the immense gratitude and respect I have for them.

By opening up Margaret's papers they are giving an enormous contribution to the study of Bletchley Park's code breaking past and the pioneering time for the first British Airborne forces during World War 2.

I give special thanks to Ian Richards, whose love and support has brought this project to fruition. He listens to hours of my ramblings about Bletchley Park and my research, then endures the ringing of the same words over and over again as I verbally assault everyone with my enthusiasm. To Redmon, my fabulous son, who has no choice but to love Bletchley Park and, at 7 years old, is showing a better understanding of the physical act of code breaking than I ever will. To Robin Howard, Maureen Howard and Julie Turner who endlessly support me especially with juggling work, writing and family life.

Also, I give my thanks to those who have contributed to the contents of this book and website. Mavis Batey, for sharing her knowledge of her colleague and life long friend, Margaret and giving an insight into what life was like at Bletchley Park; Elizabeth Batey for kindly sharing letters from her Godmother; Michael Smith, who is my hero of words, for sharing his expertise on Dilly Knox and the work carried out in Cottage No.3, Bletchley Park;

Lucinda Webb and all those at Portsmouth High School for Girls for allowing me to walk the halls as Margaret did and showing me her name in the time honoured Scholars and Examination Successes boards; Annabel Gill, archivist from Royal Holloway, who found Margaret's university records and granted me permission to reproduce them here. I cannot forget to thank Jon Cape for his generous and excellent technical and design help as well as Steve Waring, Richard Jones and Julie Turner who gave up their time to iron out some of my many grammatical errors.

A book can only succeed with an audience, and I thank all the Bletchley Park Research newsletter readers. I give extra special thanks to Wendy Appleton, Linda Bish, Brian Benedict, Brad Bunnin, Charlotte Hathaway, Rachel Hathaway, Peter Jenner, Diane Lowther, Anne Macaulay, Lara Maynard, Robert Tyson, Frode Weierud and Frank Viola who gave valuable, constructive and often fun contributions to the naming of this book. It is a small token of my appreciation that I name them here.

Last, but not least, I want to thank you for purchasing this book and giving your time to reading it. Your purchase also gives something back, as part of the book's profit will be donated to the Bletchley Park Trust, Buckinghamshire and to the Airborne Assault Museum, Duxford. It is these organisations that give a lasting and honoured home to the voices of the past. Please take the time to visit them when you can.

INTRODUCTION

Autumn was turning in to the cold British winter when I first spoke to Charles Foster, the second cousin of Margaret Rock, Bletchley Park codebreaker.

"You'll have to come up for the weekend", he said with friendly enthusiasm, *"there is too much to see in a day."* I was elated to discover that he had kept the papers belonging to his enigmatic relative.

I arrived at their home in Arley, a small rural village in Cheshire, England on 18 November 2012 and was welcomed with the warm smiles of Charles and Jane Foster. Charles, the son of Margaret's cousin, had taken the time to review Margaret's papers and arrange them chronologically. I could see piles of letters tied with string, stacked albums brimming with photographs, a box full of loose papers, photographs, sketchbooks and address books. I felt a moment of ecstatic joy - the tingling of excitement that I get when I find a treasure trove of old documents. I was the proverbial child in the sweet shop. And what tasty sweets I consumed over the next few days!

The papers I found completely changed my original goal for seeking out Margaret's family. After watching The Bletchley Circle, I was inspired to write an article about the little covered story of Bletchley's women code breakers on my website **www.bletchleyparkresearch.co.uk**. Margaret's papers changed everything.

The amazing letters laid bare the day to day lives of Margaret and her brother, John Frank Rock and it was truly a joy to read them in their original form. By bringing out a book of those letters, I hope that others will experience the same pleasure and insight that I did. Of course I can't recreate the joy of opening a small handwritten envelope, unfolding the grainy white paper and reading the words for the first time as they spilled out from the writer's mind into a black swirl of writing (sometimes legible and other times not).

I have only edited the letters where it would add to the reading experience or where parts could not be fully read. For the most part, the letters you read are as they are written. I apologise in advance for any incorrect interpretation of names and places. I have checked the spellings as much as possible.

Margaret and her brother were just ordinary people living out their lives as best they could during the challenging and painful years of World War 2. The war brought out the best in them, as it did to so many others but it also irreversibly changed their lives. For Margaret the war offered her a chance to utilise her mathematical abilities and great intellect. She had left school wanting a career in a time when the primary role for a woman was as wife and mother. The war changed the workforce, with many women recruited to cover the jobs the men left behind to protect their country.

For charismatic John, a military career was already underway by the time Britain declared war on Germany on 3rd September 1939. He excelled in the British Army's Royal Engineers so it was inevitable that he rose to the rank of great responsibility, and also great sacrifice.

He was part of the British Expeditionary Force (BEF) sent to support France. Hitler invaded Belguim on 10th May 1940 with a surprise move through the Ardenne Forest and a push through into France, taking the Allies completely unaware. The battle lasted six weeks, with German troops pushing back the Allies to the beaches of Dunkirk, where an extraordinary evacuation of troops saved over 300,000 British and French lives. A month later, John was charged with setting up the first British Paratrooper Regiment and later, as Commading Officer 1st Glider Brigade.

Both Margaret and John held roles of enormous responsibility during World War 2 but carried out their roles with humble discretion. To them it was business as usual.

Three months before her thirty-seventh birthday, Margaret was recruited by the Foreign Office to the Government Code and Cypher School's Research Section, run by the brilliant codebreaker, Dilly Knox. On 15 April 1940 Margaret arrived at Bletchley Park, the unusual mansion and sprawling grounds nestled in the Buckinghamshire countryside. Unlike many of her peers who arrived at Bletchley Park, she knew her exact destination before setting out and was able to give the postal address to her family. We can only image what Margaret thought when she took in the once quiet estate that had been undergoing a radical transformation since it had been purchased by Admiral Hugh Sinclair two years earlier for the Government Code and Cypher School and Secret Intelligence Service (MI6) in case of war.

Poised to embark on a top secret job that would focus on breaking the German Enigma machine codes, Margaret could never have foreseen that this was the start of a code breaking career that would continue until she retired from GCHQ (Government Communications Headquarters) in 1963.

Margaret treasured all of John's letters, keeping them in memory of the brother she was close to and was tragically taken from her in a Glider accident in 1942. Through his voice we learn about Margaret and her life as well as the dynamic and pioneering life he was living.

It is unfortunate that we don't have Margaret's letters to John, but with his army life, it is unlikely he had the luxury of keeping so many personal trophies. Some letters from

Margaret have survived; those written to Margaret by her mother, Alice Rock and those written by her lifelong friend, Norah Sheward. These include a fascinating first-hand account of a frightening September night in 1940 when Margaret's train was evacuated during a night of German bombing attacks.

This book is not a definitive account of Margaret or John's lives or careers. It is a mere introduction to these fair-haired heroes and a glimpse into the period of their important work during World War 2. There are many excellent books covering the key historical events briefly mentioned here. I want you, the reader, to enjoy their words in their purest form but I have added some commentary to create a backdrop in which the letters were written. I have also added more information in the accompanying website, wwww.dearcodebreaker.com, where you can find the resources that would never otherwise have made it into a book. If, like me, you instantly seek out more on the intriguing points, I have done my best to anticipate that inquisitiveness and have collated many resources for you to enjoy at your leisure. See the back of this book to find out how to get access to the exclusive material.

The extended material on the website is an experiment in multimedia book publishing. It will be updated when new material is discovered or a piece of the Bletchley Park puzzle appears relevant.

I hope you are as touched by their lives as I am and enjoy the wealth of material that appears on the evolving website to accompany this book. I would love to hear what you think of John and Margaret Rock.

Finally, remember to sign up to the dedicated newsletter for Dear Code Breaker to be the first to know when new material is added.

Go to **www.dearcodebreaker.com** and sign up now.

CHAPTER ONE

Early Years 1903 to 1916

Margaret's early years were set in the comfortable backdrop of the London District of Hammersmith, supported by the income of her father, Frank Ernest Rock, physician and surgeon working in a private practice. After serving as a Surgeon for two years in His Majesty's Royal Navy between 1894 and 1896 on ships such as the Victory, Endymion and Defiance, the large Victorian house on Glenthorne Road was the epitome of domestic comfort.

Margaret Alice Rock was born on 7 July 1903, a year into the marriage of thirty three year old Frank Ernest Rock and his younger wife by 5 years, Alice Margaret Simmonds. John Frank Rock followed two years later on 25 July 1905 and the doting parents set about documenting and photographing the lives of their children.

In 1906 the family were still living in their ten roomed house in Hammersmith. In about 1908, after a short period of work in a Huddersfield Hospital, Frank Rock moved his family to a large property with eleven rooms at Upfield, Bush Hill Road, Edmonton, Middlesex. The family employed Kate Oakes as a domestic cook and Eva Broyd as a housemaid.

At the time the area was experiencing an explosion in housing development and population growth that had continued to gain momentum from the mid 1800s. Frank was employed to oversee the medical practices in the

Edmonton elementary schools providing 14,000 local children with the first stages of their formal education.

By the time the 1911 Census was underway Margaret was still living at home with her parents, but the tradition of sending a child away to school was on the horizon and Margaret was soon sent to the nearby North Middlesex School.

During Margaret's four years at North Middlesex School, she met and befriended Norah Frances Sheward, her senior in age by two days. Between the walls of this boarding school for girls, Margaret and Norah forged the foundation of a friendship that lasted their lifetime and was strengthened in later years when both were single women looking after elderly parents.

It would have been during Margaret's years at North Middlesex School that her father Frank was called back into the Royal Navy. In December 1903 he had been placed on a list of volunteers prepared to serve in the event of war or an emergency. Despite his physical absence, Frank kept in regular contact with his wife and children, always ready to encourage and nurture the growing educational talents of his offspring. The hard work and advice paid off - in 1916 Margaret passed her Cambridge Local Exam including honours in History.

In about 1916 Alice moved with the children to Colchester, where Margaret and John attended separate schools . With her husband away, Alice had no need to maintain the roots they had set down in Edmonton. Instead she chose to stay close to her children.

Margaret Alice Rock & John Frank Rock as children

Frank Ernest Rock 1914

Frank Rock
20 Queen Anne's Grove
Bush Hill Park

30 April 1914

Miss Rock
Sandringham House
Frinton on Sea

My Dear Margaret,

Thank you for your nice long letter. I was very glad to get it this morning with that of Mummy's.

I am so glad you are enjoying yourself. I have no doubt you get out every minute of the day that you are able to. Fancy persuading Mother to take off her shoes and stockings and paddling. Tell her she ought to know better. Whatever will Jimmy do with a dog and a cat in the house. If the cat doesn't fight him I expect the dog will, or perhaps they will both make love to Jimmy and get jealous of each other and fight. It would be a pity for Jimmy to come and make them enemies. He is awfully lonely without you. He is always going to the window to look out and see if you are coming.

We didn't have a fire at all yesterday. But this evening as I was having dinner it felt a little chilly, and I thought I should enjoy my cigar and a glass of port after dinner better in front of a nice fire, so here I am drinking a glass of port and smoking a cigar and writing to you all at the same time.

We had a bad thunderstorm last night, and today it has been raining on and off, and tonight it is really pouring.

Mr Forbes came in to see me this evening and we had a little talk and then he went on to see someone else.

The paper in this letter is for Mummy.

Give Mummy a kiss for me and also John. I am so looking forward to coming and seeing you.

From Your Loving Father

Frank Rock
Royal Naval Barracks
Chatham

18 May 1914

Master John Rock
44 North Hill
Colchester

My Dear John,

I am writing to you this time first, as I wrote to Margaret I think last. I have now a nice room in the barracks, larger I think than our bedroom at home.

I have my bicycle from Uncle Arthur and had it cleaned up, but the first time I rode it I had a puncture and had to leave it at the shop again and have it mended, but I managed to have a little ride first through the country lanes. It is very pretty indeed when you get off the main road, the fruit trees are all full of blossom.

It must have been very intimidating to see the review, I wish I could have been there with you. I hope to be able to see you next Saturday, but I shall have to leave again on Sunday, it is not long, is it?

I am expecting to see Grandma and Grandpa soon. I think they are coming today.

I hope you are getting on well at school.

With love to Mother, Margaret and yourself from

Your Loving Father

Frank Rock
Royal Naval Barracks
Chatham

7 July 1914

My Dear Margaret,

Will you tell Mother that I got her letter this morning. Also tell her that I replied to her telegram at once. Telegrams as well as letters take a long time to travel over such a long distance.

It seems such a long time since I left Whitley Bay, Mother has told me that you have been in the sea. Did you find it very cold? You must not go out of your depth, if I am not with you and if you did, you might get too tired before you got into your depth again.

The first two nights I was here I had to sleep on the mattress put on the floor. They have taken so many beds away as they could for the hospital. They expect to have a lot of wounded men here soon. War is a dreadful thing, isn't it? But this war we can't help, and it was our duty to go into it, as everyone must do his best.

I have not been able to go and [see] Uncle Arthur or Auntie Connie because everyone has to stay in barracks in case they are wanted.

This place is full of sailors and officers and they all have a lot to do.

With love to John and you and Grandpa and Grandma and to Mother from

Your Loving Father

Frank Rock
Royal Naval Barracks
Chatham

17 July 1914

Miss Rock
20 Queen Anne's Grove
Bush Hill Park
Enfield

My Dear Margaret,

I was very glad to get your letter this morning and hear your news. Of course I was quite certain that being first meant first distinguished. Will you please tell mother that I got the boots this morning and I am very much obliged to her for sending them. I have them on now and they are so comfortable.

We have had today a little game of pretending. We pretended that a ship had come to the dockyard with a lot of wounded men, and we had a lot of cots and made a lot of men, who where really quite well but pretended to be be wounded, lie down in them, and we put them into ambulances and I went to the hospital with them, and then we came back and took another lot of men who pretended to be wounded to hospital and then I took a cab and came back here, got off my uniform and had a walk through the town and now I am back waiting for dinner. A funny game wasn't it. And the inside of the ambulance was so hot and stuffy.

I often see here Mr Ralph Marwood, a brother of the Doctor Marwood that we went to see at Portsmouth last year.

Well goodbye dear, love to you and John and Mummie and don't forget Jimmie. What a pity that Dickie is so disgraceful.

Your Loving Father
F.E Rock

Margaret Rock
Douglas Square
Newcastleton

18 July 1914

Dear Daddy,

I hope you are having a nice time at Aberdeen. We are having a lovely time here. This morning we went out with Uncle Herbert. We escorted him, and had a lovely time.

The weather has improved, and the sun was shining in the morning. In a few minutes we will go to make hay. We will take our tea with us.

With love from

Margaret

Frank Rock
Royal Naval Barracks
Chatham

21 July 1914

My Dear John,

I was very glad to get your letter. You write so nicely that I must try and write nicely too. I was very glad to hear that both you and Margaret did so will at swimming on Saturday. Now you will be able to enjoy the sea so much better than if you could not swim at all.

Mummy tells me that Birdie is not well. I am so sorry and do hope that she will soon be better. She has sent me also an account of your new school, and I think that you will like it very much.

I am looking forward very much to seeing you all again as I miss you very much.

Your Loving Father

F.E.Rock

Frank Rock
HMS Wallaroo
C/O GPO

28 December 1914

Miss Rock
1 Beach Road
Clacton on Sea

My Dear Margaret

Thank you very much for your Christmas card. I think you draw Jimmy splendidly. The attitude in which he was sitting is quite like him, and I think you have got him just right.

I said goodbye to Mummie in Cannon St. Station this afternoon, and very sorry I was too. We had a lovely two days together and it seemed very short, and still we managed to do a great deal. We saw Auntie Mabel; had dinner with Grandpa John and Auntie Ethel and Julie on Saturday. On Sunday we saw Mr & Mrs Jun, , had lunch with Mr an Mrs Alderton, had tea with Dr and Mrs Young, and had supper with Mr Keyer at the Frascah's restaurant. I do wish you and John had been there. It was a lovely place, beautifully decorated and with lots of enormous crackers all over the place, and people all well dressed.

Will you tell Mummie that the box of cigars was here when I arrived and I had one and enjoyed it very much.

It is blowing here tonight quite as badly as it ever did at Clacton. What it is like at Clacton I don't know, but I should think that it was more windy tonight that it has ever been before.

Do you know that on Christmas Day the German Aeroplane passed right over our heads going up the river and again coming down, but it did not try do us any harm at all. When it passed us going back we saw the guns firing at it and the shells bursting close beside it, and then we finally saw it going away to the north.

Well dear goodbye and good night. I hope this dreadful wind will not keep you awake all night, with love to you and John and Mummie too.

Your loving father

Frank Rock

A little kiss for Jimmie, and also love to Uncle and Auntie.

Frank Rock
HMS Wallaroo

Saturday 1915

Miss Rock
30 Eversly Road
Bexhill

My Dear Margaret

I return you your exercises. The maps I think are very well done. I have put in one or two names that you might remember. They are certain to come up during the war. Mother will tell you all about Venice for she has been there.

Now will you look at the map and tell me which is the most northerly, and southern most and the western most point in Europe.

The enclosed is for mother. I had a letter from Uncle Herbert yesterday. He thought you were looking well. I hope you are all enjoying yourselves.

We find it very monotonous here.

With love from

Your loving Father

Frank Ernest Rock served on the Wallaroo from 4 December 1914 to 1 May 1916. It is estimated that this letter was sent in 1915 as it bears the same address and is similarly marked to a postcard of the Wallaroo Frank sent to Margaret on the 14th of either June or July 1915.

John Rock
44 North Hill
Colchester
Essex

30 January 1916

Dear Father

I was fourth this week, rather good wasn't it seeing there are thirty-two boys in my class, you see the first and second have been put together, not counting ten new boys. We had a School Concert yesterday evening, I went and sung and Margaret and mother looked on. I am sure you will like the new house, it is so new and neat, you would have laughed at us sometimes. I am sure if you could have seen Mother drying and Margaret washing the things up, while I blacked the boots, by myself, and my apron, which was the bottom of one of Margaret's dresses, rolled a good many times round me.

Our first dinner turned out very well, it was meat, sprouts and fried potatoes, with a lot of gravy. Yesterday we got a servant who is a very good cook, but before that mother had to do the cooking, and us the laying of the table, and the reading, because there is a case full of very interesting books.

With love from

John Frank Rock

Frank Rock
HMS Laurentic

Friday November 1916

My Dear Margaret,

I was very glad to get yours and John's letters. I am answering yours now, and will write to John next week. It seemed a long time time to wait to join my ship, and I am very glad to be here at last. It is a large ship and there are a lot of officers, quite 40; very different to the old Walleroo isn't it, where there were only six of us. I have got a very comfortable cabin, in fact two cabins. There is a nice wardroom which we only use for meals, and a large smoking room. This used to be the ladies drawing room when the ship was a passenger ship, and it is comfortably furnished with nicely upholstered easy chairs and sofas. There is also another smoking room not so well furnished where there is a piano. It is here that people go when they want to make a noise and have games. The piano is not a good one. It has had lots of hard work and thumping, and is much smaller than the ordinary piano, so that if there are high notes or low notes in the music you have to stop. Still its better than nothing.

I was very interested to hear about your Cambridge Local. I think you will get through alright, but am afraid you will have a lot of work before Christmas, and you will thankfully deserve your Christmas Holiday. I suppose they give you specimen papers at the school. They might do, because it will give you practice in answering papers, and enable you to judge how much time you have for answering. Always read the question very carefully before starting to answer it, and in the sums be quite certain that you have got it down right. Don't be in too much of a hurry, because that is how you make mistakes, but at the same time don't dawdle and above all try to leave yourself plenty of time at the end so that you can look through your answers, if possible; also it is very awkward to leave yourself no time for the last two or three questions. If there is a question you are quite at sea about leave it and go on to the next. It is very likely that while you are doing the rest of the paper the answer to the question you didn't know will come to you. Be careful to write plainly especially figures and the letters in geometry.

In French, always read the passage to be translated from French to English very carefully through, perhaps twice before you start to translate. Reading it through will often give you the general idea of the piece; and the translation from French to English very often gives you very valuable hints to help you in the translation from English to French.

Never give up. If a question or paper seems hard always answer it even if you do it imperfectly. Some questions are so hard that the examiners don't expect perfection; and you may have done very well, when you think you have done badly. Be confident, but not over confident for that often causes rashness.

There, I have given you a lot of advice, and hope it will help you. I think you will get through and hope not very horribly disappointed if you don't. It will be a great feather in your cap if you do, but if you don't you can always go up again. I shall be very glad to hear from you afterwards to know if you enjoy examinations. I think there is something sporting about them, and there is always a certain element of chance.

I think you have done very well in your class, and so has John.

We are having beautiful weather. Today it is colder. I have my electric heater on all night. Then I can do with less bed clothes; and it is very nice going to a bathroom which is heated.

I have a cold bath and, it is salt water, and then I have a shower bath afterwards, cold fresh water which washes all the salt water off, and then I feel beautifully warm and glowing and tingly.

Well dear I think I have written you a nice long letter. Tell John I will write to him in a day or two. My best love to you both from

Your loving Father

Frank Rock served on HMS Laurentic from 23 September 1916. He lost his life aboard the ship when it struck a German mine off the coast of Ireland on 25 January 1917.

CHAPTER TWO

Getting Ahead in Education
1917 - 1925

With two children at school and a husband serving his country as a naval surgeon, Alice Rock spent most of 1914 to 1917 without a long term address, never settling while away from the close family unit she depended on. This changed in 1917 when Alice moved to Portsmouth, returning to her husband's childhood town. It was time to set down some roots and find a school for fourteen year old Margaret.

Once settled at 4 Woodpath, Southsea, Margaret enrolled at Portsmouth High School for Girls, a growing independent school with 171 students in 1917.

According to her school record Margaret had spent the previous years at private boarding school (North Middlesex School, Enfield for four years and Endleigh House, Colchester for one and a quarter years). Margaret's attended Portsmouth High School as a day student, returning daily to her mother at 4 Woodpath Road, then 1 Taswell Road, Southsea where they remained throughout Margaret's time at Portsmouth High School.

Portsmouth High School was set up in 1881 by the Girls Day School Company in response to the need for a girls school to cater for the offspring of the wealthy Portsmouth businessmen during a time of growing dissatisfaction in education generally. Schools geared towards educating the young ladies of 'gentlemen' did not consider these businessmen to fit into gentile society, so despite being able to pay the fees, the girls were turned away with a sniff of snobbery.

Supported by education campaigner, Canon Grant (who was also the Vicar of Portsmouth), and spearheaded by Mr W.J. Edmonds (an accountant keen to secure good education for his daughters), a successful approach was made to the Girls Day School Company and the development of Portsmouth High School was soon underway.

On 21 February 1882 thirty girls walked into the "*plain and sturdy*" school of red brick that was considered by a reporter for the Portsmouth Times to be '*a commodious and well situated building*'. The headmistress of this era was a Miss Ledger, a determined woman with a clear vision on how to steer the foundling years of the school against a backgound of local criticism and snobbery. As well as their education, Miss Ledger kept a careful eye on the deportment of her girls, even forbidding them to even touch the handrails as they went up and down the stairs.

Miss Ledger was the first of many headmistresses that encouraged the few girls who wished to have a career. It was twelve years after the school was founded that with the encouragement of Miss Ledger, Lily Flowers was the first Portsmouth High School student to go to university, where she read Mathematics at Newnham College, Cambridge.

Newnham College was to be the training ground of Miss Ada Cossey, the Headmistress of Portsmouth High School during Margaret Rock's school years. Miss Ledger, Miss Adamson and Miss Steele guided the school until Miss Cossey's formidable and legendary reign from 1908 to 1932.

Miss Cossey was also a Newnham College graduate and was a strong and guiding light during her tenure as headmistress between 1908 and 1932. The school expanded under her guidance and she ensured the girls experienced a culture within the school that was rich and varied. The girls also achieved great academic success. Miss Cossey encouraged the adventurous and cultured pursuits of her students, but actively discouraged idle socialising.

'I do want to urge upon the parents that they should not let their girls time and energy be taken up by social pleasures during the school week. This is a place where the passion for amusement is exceptionally keen and where there are endless opportunities for indulging in it. Parties, theatre-going, performances at bazaars, picture-palaces are sad hindrances with school-girls to repose, good health and steady work, and they encourage in unformed natures much that needs checking and not encouraging.'

Miss Cossey's educational principles of hard work and encouragement of more desirable pursuits of sport, drama and school societies gave rise to great educational success within the school. It was an excellent environment for Margaret to develop her abilities and find her passion for mathematics.

As the war raged on, the decision to change Margaret's school may have been financial. John's path was already settled, he would continue to receive a military education at the Imperial Service College, Windsor and Royal Military Academy, Sandhurst, graduating into The British Army's Royal Engineers in 1925. John's education fees were a cost that would have to continue.

When Margaret enrolled at Portsmouth High School for Girls on 17 January 1917, her father's ship (HMS Laurentic) was docked in Liverpool preparing its cargo of 35 tons of gold, equating to £5 million at that time and in 2009 was worth an estimated £750 million. The gold was making a vital journey across the freezing winter swells of the Atlantic Ocean to Halifax, Novia Scotia to pay for munitions.

HMS Laurentic was chosen for its speed and ability to slip through the net of prowling German U-boats, but on the evening of 25 January 1917 the ship triggered a mine set by U-Boat, U80. Twenty seconds later another explosion on the port side sealed the Laurentic's fate. Within forty five minutes, having dumped its crew and cargo into the icy grey sea, the Laurentic sank. Of the 475 men on board, 354 perished, some from the explosions but most from exposure while waiting for rescue.

Despite the massive salvage project between 1917 and 1924, during which the Admiralty retrieved 3,186 bars of gold, some of the 25 bars unaccounted for remain buried in the silty grave of the Laurentic wreck.

Margaret's first days at school as a lower fifth student were marred by grief for the father she loved and who had encouraged and nurtured her intellect. In hindsight, there must have been some sense of relief in the choice of keeping Margaret close to home, for as a day school student she was home daily to console and be consoled by her mother.

Despite an pension and a private income of £560, Alice Rock was able to secure a grant towards Margaret's estimated £28 per annum education costs. The Girls Day School Trust awarded a scholarship of £6 per year for the two years Margaret was a Junior and £9 - £10 per year for her two years as a Senior at Portsmouth High School.

Despite her grief during the start of her time at school, Margaret went on to pass the London General School Exam with matriculation exemption in June 1919. This was the first year the new Higher School Certificate was introduced and although 28,800 students took the exam, it did not guarantee an automatic university place for those who wished to pursue further study. Only those students who achieved a higher level of achievement by obtaining a matriculation exemption were able to progress into a university education.

Margaret obtained honours in French, Mathematics and Music and opted to continue studying French and Mathematics as part of her Bachelor of Arts (B.A) Degree at Bedford College, University of London. Bedford College came under the umbrella of the University of London in 1900 and merged with another of the university's colleges, Royal Holloway in 1982.

Only a small number of women entered into university in the first quarter of the 1900s. In 1920 only 1,212 women achieved a first degree compared to 3,145 men. By 1930 this had grown to 2,635 women compared to 6,494 men. It appears that of all university degrees, approximately one third were obtained by women up to the 1970s, when there was a fifty percent split. From the year 2000 the number of women obtaining degrees surpassed the number of their male peers.

In 1849, at the age of sixty Mrs Elizabeth Jesser Reid invested £1,500 using the private income from her late husband and parents to turn a childhood dream of '*a College for women or something like it*' into a reality. Mrs Reid had a vision of improving the joy of a woman's life by enhancing their skills with knowledge of literature, history and science. She believed this knowledge would make these women '*better wives and more understanding mothers.*' As a social activist and anti-slavery reformer, Mrs Reid was no stranger to testing the conventions of the day. Bedford College of 47 Bedford Square, London, was the first college of higher education for women in the country.

After Mrs Reid's death in 1866 Bedford College changed under the direction of three assertive female trustees who guided it into an establishment offering a high standard of academic education for women with external examinations and its own constitution.

By the time Margaret started in the Autumn of 1921 there were approximately 640 students. The previous year the college had decided to only accept students who had matriculated, and by 1923 there was an entrance exam. Margaret was fortunate to receive an 'exhibition', meaning she was exempt from paying her fees if she had reached certain grades. Professor Harold Hilton and Miss Fanny Cecilia Johnson were her tutors in Mathematics and French respectively.

It was at Bedford College that Margaret was able to explore her love of mathematics and numbers. Examining her school reports, it is clear that the theoretical academic study started to take its toll on her enthusiasm and it was not until later that her language and mathematics talent were exploited in a more practical way.

Engineer Rear Admiral Mogg
Beechcroft
Alverstoke
Hants

22 July 1920

The Principal
Bedford College for Women
London

Dear Madam,

In reply to your letter, I consider Miss M.A. Rock in all respects suitable for admission as a student, She appears to me to be clever and studious and would, I believe, be a credit to the College.

I have known her family many years.

Yours faithfully

Engineer Rear Admiral W.G. Mogg

Engineer Rear Admiral William George Mogg was appointed to The Most Honourable Order of the Bath on 1 January 1919 for his service during World War 1.

Mary Tuke
Principal
Bedford College

28 October 1920

Dear Mrs Rock,

I have pleasure in informing you that the Council at their meeting yesterday warded your daughter an Exhibition for the session 1921-1922, which will admit her to the College for the course of instruction in preparation for the B.A. degree without payment of tuition fees.

The Exhibition is awarded in the first instance for one year but will be renewed so as to enable your daughter to enter for the Final B.A Examination not later than October 1925 subject to satisfactory reports on her work and progress each session.

Yours truly

Principal

Mary J. Tuke, Principal of Bedford College from 1907 to 1929

Alice Rock
1 Taswell Road
Southsea

29 October 1920

Dear Madam,

Will you kindly convey my very grateful thanks to your Committee for awarding my daughter an Exhibition for the first year of her University course. I am sure she will do her utmost to satisfy them that it will not be given in vain.

Yours faithfully

Alice M. Rock

Miss Tuke
Principal
Bedford College

6 July 1922

Dear Miss Rock,

You will already know that your names appears on the list of successful candidates in the intermediate Arts Examinations.

I am writing to tell you that you have been recommended to read for an Honours degree in Mathematics and to take the examinations in 1925. The Final Examination in that year will begin on the third Monday in June.

Yours sincerely

Principal

Margaret Rock
Rosslyn
Queen's Road
Thame
Oxon

14 July 1922

Dear Miss Tuke,

I was very glad to receive your letter which was awaiting me when I arrived home. Will you please thank the Council very much for renewing the Exhibition I received last session.

I am very glad that I am allowed to read for a Maths: Honours Degree. Mother is very grateful for the decision of the Council.

Yours sincerely

Margaret Rock

Margaret continued to receive the exhibition throughout her studies at Bedford College.

John Rock
Imperial Service College
Windsor

1 March 1923

Miss M.A. Rock
75 Boundary Road
London
N.W.8

My Dear Margaret,

These have come at last. This is the 1st XV, and you won't have much difficulty in placing me.

I hope you are well and enjoying yourself. The Junior Cross Country was run this afternoon. A house second.

Love from John

After graduating from the Imperial Service College, John starts at the Royal Military Academy, Woolwich on 31 August 1923

John Rock is second from the right in the middle row.

CHAPTER THREE

Adventurous Adults
1926- 1938

There is very little information about Margaret's career after leaving Bedford College. According to her relative, Charles Foster, Margaret was a statistician employed by the National Association of Manufacturers or Federation of British Industry (which were later combined with the British Employers Confederation to form the Confederation of British Industry).

Margaret told Charles she produced forecasts on the economy and how different sectors of manufacturing would perform. Given Margaret's maths skill, this would have been an ideal job, especially as in the 1920s she had decided against teaching as a profession. As yet, Margaret's career remains an area to be explored further.

What is known is that it was a period of great adventure and freedom. Margaret never married and had an additional private income of £50 per annum from an inheritance.

Photograph albums show many trips abroad with her mother and others with her brother, John. These trips included visits to friends and family in Great Britain, a tour of Italy, skiing in Switzerland and France, and a trip to visit John in Ceylon (now Sri Lanka). With no husband to tend to, Margaret was free to travel.

John had not married either, instead he enjoyed his developing career. During this period he climbed the ranks in the Royal Engineers, where his promotion to Acting Lieutenant in November 1928 was formalised in March 1929. Shortly after a three month language course in German in March 1933, John was halfway to his promotion to Captain, a rank he finally attained on 3 September 1936

From December 1934 John was the Aide De Camp to the Commander in Charge of the International Force posted in the Saar Territory. The Saar Territory is an area in Germany that had been under British governance since 1920. Change was underway by the time John arrived and on 1 March 1935, the governance of the territory was handed over to the Thrid Reich. John arranged for the removal of forces from the area and returned home on 16 March 1934.

By the end of April, John was redeployed, this time to Ceylon as Officer in Charge of the 31st Coy. He wrote many descriptive letters from Ceylon, evoking a hot, humid life of food, travel and sport. John preferred to talk about more social aspects of his life and only lightly touched upon his work duties in these letters.

By 1938 John was at the School of Mechanical Engineers, Chatham and in January 1939 embarked on a short appointment as an instructor in construction at the school.

John's enjoyment of his work and life is obvious and comes across in his lively letters to Margaret and Alice.

Margaret Rock
22b Barmsole Road
Gillingham
Kent

1 February [circa 1926]

Dear Miss Haydon,

Thank you very much for your letter dated Dec 28th. It seems terrible, not answering it before, but unfortunately I only received it a day or so ago. We left Boundary Road over a year ago, and have never had a permanent address since.

It was awfully good of you to let me know of the vacant post. I have decided that I am not going to teach, however, so I would not have applied for it in any case, but thank you very much for writing.

Yours sincerely

Margaret Rock

The Electoral Register shows that Alice Rock was living in Boundary Road in 1925. There is no confirmed address for Alice or Margaret until 1927, when they are recorded at 30 St. Mary's Mansions - an address they lived until 1934.

The address in Gillingham is near to John, who was studying at the School for Mechanical Engineers, Chatham after receiving a commission in the Royal Engineers on 3 September 1925. Once Margaret had completed her studies, there was nothing to hold them in London and once again, Alice moved the family to keep her children close by.

Margaret Rock
22b Barmsole Road
Gillingham
Kent

22 February [circa 1926]

Dear Miss Haydon,

Thank you very much for your letter I received this morning. I think the post you mentioned sounds very interesting, and I have written to Miss Brown about it.

We have given up trying to get a flat while living here, so are coming to London for good on Friday, when our address will be Bayswater Court, St. Stephen's Road, Bayswater, W.2, but I hope I shall have a really permanent address soon.

Yours sincerely

Margaret Rock

Margaret Rock
P.Ack Herrn Dr Rylinzka
St Anton am Arlberg
Tirol Austria

Sunday 2 February 1930
5.30pm

My dear Mother,

Herewith an account of our journey and arrival. We got here at 2.40 this afternoon and there is several inches of snow - just enough to ski on, but I expect higher up it is better. It has been a glorious day, with a bright blue sky and wonderful sunshine.

To begin at the beginning we got to Dover very comfortably, with heaps of time and got on board before anyone else. The boat was nearly empty, and the sea was rather rough. We had our lunch before the boat started, and later went and had some coffee in the bar, and sat there the whole time as it was nice and warm. Going down to Dover we passed through a fearful storm of snow and hail. The car felt almost as if it would be blown over. We managed very well at Ostend, carrying our own luggage, and discovered that we would have one and a quarter hours at Brussels, the train leaving at 7 o'clock. We decided to have dinner at Brussels and left our luggage in the train and gave the guard 5 frs (swiss). We went into a large and cheap-looking restaurant exactly opposite the hotel Albert and had a very good dinner. Veal steak with mushrooms, salad and potatoes, and John had Camembert cheese and a lemon cake. All very good and well cooked and plenty of it, especially the meat (which we finished, nevertheless). Also lashings of rolls and butter. We had 3 beers between us and it cost all that was left of the Belgian money (less than 6/-). Later in the evening we had a light coffee and an aspirin each.

We had a carriage to ourselves the whole night and spread our legs across the seats and used our rucksacks as pillows and were quite comfortable. The drawback was that the train stopped so often we could hardly get asleep, but the last 3 hours were better, with only 3 stops. We got to Basel almost on time (4.50 by Greenwich time, but really 5.00) and each had a leisurely bath and breakfast - caught our 7.40 in comfort. Unfortunately, the only through coach was only first and second class so we had to have several changes (3 to be exact) but we really didn't mind an occasional stroll at all; in fact, it was such a lovely day we enjoyed them. We had lunch in a long wait so we have had no meals on the trains, but much cheaper and pleasanter ones. I certainly have never felt so well after a long train journey and made a good lunch and probably will a good dinner (ditto John).

Frau Rylinzka made us a cup of tea when we arrived, which I much appreciated as I was dying of thirst. Otherwise, we are giving our insides a rest til dinner. Mine needs it - it suffered after the good lunch (soup, slices of beef, salad, potato chips and brussel sprouts and cheese) (3 frs)(and a glass of beer, very cheap).

I felt very tired when we arrived but we have been strolling about the village for some time, and I feel quite full of life again, and not a bit as tired as I should. There is something stimulating in the air, it seems to take away all weariness. We couldn't ski, as our skis are being waxed, won't be ready til tomorrow morning.

NOW very important John has left behind his spongebag with contents and his shaving tackle. I have forgotten to buy a dressing gown, and would like two more pairs of shoe trees. We should be awfully grateful if you would make a parcel and send it off as soon as possible, either the silk Japanese dressing gown or the pink will do, and John's things are in the bathroom. He has just been shaved at the Friseur's.

He joins me in love from Margaret

John, Margaret & Friend skiing 1930

Alice Rock
30 St Marys Mansions
Paddington
W.2

6 February 1930
Thursday afternoon

My Dearest Margaret,

I can tell you it was a lovely surprise to get your letters last night. I did not think the post was as quick.

My word, Tuesday was the longest day I have ever known. By the evening I fancied you had been gone a week and now it seems ages since Monday.

Tonight will be my first evening at home. What a pathetic cry "as much grass" and from the paper not much has changed. Awful hard luck, you don't seem to have had cheerful a night journey, pity you could not be alone; but even then the stopping would have bothered you. What a disappointment to have fair and how different to John's journey last year, when the windows were frosty. I feel that your wardrobe is not equipped for so much walking, you can't go about in your skiing suit if you can't ski. I hope the skating was a success. I am sorry you are paying 22 francs. I have already sent on the letter but it was not definitive. You must be on at them about changing or they will keep you in their rooms.

Yesterday afternoon it turned much colder and is so today. The wind is bitter, it was sunny but very cold. I feel hopeful for you. You would have enjoyed the concert on Tuesday, it was lovely. The harpsichord was more harp than piano. She got a lot out of it but the violinist was superb. They were rather new to England, at least neither spoke English during my supper. Betty phoned up, "if the concert was that night and was it evening dress". I said yes then she asked "could they come as they were?" I said, of course they could if they felt that way and did not mind being the only ones in evening dress. Then she said "they would dress" and they both looked very nice and appeared to enjoy it very much. Mrs B had a cold. It was a dry night and I walked both ways.

After phoning Miss Stevenson I went there yesterday afternoon very early, she sent her assistant matron to meet me. It was a long way to the hospital, directly I arrived she said I must stay to dinner so I phoned Maisie to postpone the hot roast. We had such talks of old times and all that has happened in twenty two years. She told a few tales of you and father, one was that he often played the piano until 2am and she asked the nurses if it did not disturb them! And they said "no indeed and if we wake up and hear the music we like it as we don't mind waking up". Just like him wasn't it? The tea was a real spread and a very good dinner followed with claret to assist. The assistant matron mealed with us, she was young and awfully nice, also Scottish and a doctor came in for coffee afterwards (male.) One was Dr Gavin, Adele's friend, he is a young man and very shy. Miss S has awfully nice quarters, a spare bedroom for her friends, to which I am invited later on, her own bathroom and usual office and an office and her sitting room, it was a very pretty room and she had a lovely embroidered little cloth for dinner. She insisted on taking me to the station and ordering a taxi which she would not let me pay for, even half! And I heard the man ask for 5/-! Really she couldn't do enough for me. Today I am doing nothing in particular and tomorrow I have Dorothy coming for tea. I haven't had a needle in my hand since you left. There will be congestion soon!

While I am writing it has started to sleet, it is quite cold in the room.

Don't forgot to go to Uncle's on Monday February 10th and to Adele's on the Friday after February 14th and home on the Monday. Adele's address is 90 London Road, St Leonards on Sea.

I have not had letters from anyone. I do hope your next letter will tell of the nursery slopes.

My love to you. Your loving Mother

Alice. M. Rock

I am writing John a line in a letter I am forwarding.

Alice Rock
30 St Mary's Mansions
W2

18th February 1930
Tuesday afternoon

My dearest Margaret

You are both awfully good to send me as many letters! It sounds wonderful to hear you talking of the heat of the sun. I can only talk of the cutting north-east wind, we have had it for days. At Hastings the sun shone brilliantly all day, but you feel the wind just the same. Yesterday afternoon we had a shower of snow. It was as cold that the snow looked just like hard, white peas and melted on the road, after ten minutes the sun came out as good as ever.

We walked to the church in the good Sunday morning sunshine. I enjoyed it and the service was delightful. We enjoyed Monsieur [...] on Saturday afternoon, his playing was beautiful, we had splendid reserved seats for 2/4. In the evening a mother and daughter came in for bridge, they said they loved it. They had no more idea of how to play than the cat. I never spent such a wasted evening.

Monday Adele went off for the day and I spent the time sitting in sheltered spots on the front. I came back by the 5 to 9 train and had supper at Hills [...] Charing X. They are clean, I bought tea, fried fish and chips and pint 2/6. It wasn't good enough carrying my bag further after the intense cold of Adele's rooms and the flat felt lonely though no fire at all in it, so much linoleum in this weather nearly killed me, I have lots of chilblains but they will go now.

Today I have been to Humly, came back to Marble Arch and had lunch at Mackies' and walked home, doing a lot of ordering and shopping on the way. The stove has been alright since 10am but I can't get the room up to 60 yet. Since writing so far I have just had John's letter with snaps, they are awfully good - awfully nice of you both. His letter explains why you had two days rest. Poor things both to have accidents, nasty ones too, I hope you are not taxing the knee too much, what an awful bump you must have given it. Poor John, was it his left hand I wonder; while it was bad he couldn't get along at all I should think. I hope the doctor is efficient. So glad the fancy dress ball was good fun, I hope you will have a real good last week. I fancy John hasn't enjoyed it like Klosters, but you have had bad luck in the weather. I am longing for you to come back - it seems a very long time now. So many things to ask you. I enjoyed my stay with Adele very much. I am sitting over the fire, hence the writing. Do you want any money sent out?

My love to you both. Your loving Mother

Alice. M. Rock

John Rock
Saar Force HQ
Eichhorn Staden
Saarbrüchen

Saturday 29 December 1934

Dear Mother,

Many thanks for your letters, the last I got this morning, enclosing several letters, which I shall play in due course.

I now have time to spread myself and try and give you some of the news.

To start with my journey here. I had a first class warrant all the way and traveled really very comfortably. I did not have to change on my way to Dover, I caught the passenger steam to Calais. The sea was fairly calm and we arrived to time, just before one of the train ferries, which was bringing M.T Column over. I found Cochran at Calais, he had been Transport Officer there for three days and he and I traveled up here together. He is now Movement Control Officer at the Railway Station here. He was one of the members of our bridge four at the Shop. I had a very late lunch at Calais and were caught a 5.30 train to Paris, arriving 9.15. All our luggage we registered free, and there were no customs or passports. We were leaving Paris at midnight, so we took a taxi to the Rue Royal, where we had a magnificent dinner in a first class restaurant. You may imagine how we were stared at. We had a carriage to ourselves all the way here and I slept a little, stretched out. We were greeted continental fashion and was handed over to one Captain Pidsley. The rest of the day was spent tearing round in taxis, looking for quarters, buying furniture, waiting in offices etc and in the evening a conference lasting until 11pm. I was ready to drop.

The next three or four days were rather similar and I can't remember exactly what happened. The usual procedure was to go round with an underling of the Ministry of the Interior; we would inspect prospective quarters and he would argue for hours with the owner about the price. I would then go to the office and make a written demand for it. The Ministry would then argue again about the cost and finally say we could move in.

The delays and prevarications were incredible and heartbreaking. I believe every member had to get his rake off. However, I got all the troops settled in and now all the officers are in billets.

We chose an Officer's Mess and thought we had the matter settled, and then found that the ground floor was let to a Dutchman till Jan 1st, so we can't move in till then, but another officer, Major Broomhall, of my Corps and myself are in billets on the first floor. I have a magnificent large room with a lot of cupboard accommodation and am very comfortable. I only spent six days in the Excelsior. It was expensive there, but we got 30f a day allowance and now get 5f a day to feed ourselves till the Mess opens. I am running the mess of course.

My work is already getting light and I think I shall be very bored if I ever have not much to do.

The people are indifferent to us. They are not particularly friendly, but are not at all hostile. I very much doubt if we will have any trouble.

I feed now with Pidsley and Broomhall in a private house for 6.50 a meal. Today I had tea for the first time. The tea shops are very fine but everything is expensive.

I have heard that there is good skiing with 100 miles and must make more detailed inquiries. I get hardly any exercise at all.

Please thank M for her letter. I have heard from Herbert and Jean. They said they had read in the paper what a magnificent Xmas we had. Actually we worked all the morning and had the afternoon off. We bought a couple of bottle of champagne and drank them at supper.

I got the troops some Xmas puddings, fruit etc for their Xmas dinner. We work official hours, 9am till 6pm with half holiday on Sunday.

I am very glad to hear you have got Tony back again, he must have been awfully lonely. What a muddle about my trunks. That fool Aunt must have sent the whole damn lot off.

I am writing this in my office this evening and must now return to my billet (close by) for a bath.

Your loving son

John

John Rock
HQ Saarforce
Sarrbrucken

Thursday 17 January 1935

Mrs Rock
Beacon Field
Windmill Hill
Nr Hailsham
Sussex

Dear Mother,

Just a line to let you know that a letter has just come through from the War Office to say that I will not be proceeding to India this Trooping Season. When the Saar Force returns I am to report back to Chatham and await orders from the War Office as to my disposal.

I thought you would like to know right away. I am now all for getting home as early as possible.

It has poured all day and is milder and the snow is slowly disappearing. Everything went off very smoothly. On the day it was announced there were great rejoicings, of course, and I sat by the phone in H all the evening in case the police want to call the troops out, but there was no trouble. I have much less to do already and shall soon have very little. I am beginning to make dispositions for leaving.

You said in your last letter, that you have paid Crawford, so have I. You must not let Margaret starve Tony, he is used to a lot of swill every day.

Sorry no more, urgent mission

Love from John

John Rock
HQ Saarforce
Sarrbrucken

20 February 1935

Mrs Rock
Beacon Field
Windmill Hill
Nr Hailsham
Sussex

Dear Ma,

I'm afraid I kept you waiting for a long time for my last letter, so I now write to repair the deficiency. I shall be arriving in London on the afternoon of Feb 28 or possibly the evening and shall repair first to Wellington BHS to take over from the Assistant Camp Commandant who will be waiting there to take over from me and then I shall go to 132 Westbourne Terrace, where I shall be very grateful if you would book a room for me. I expect to be in London at least a week, but shall not have very much to do.

I leave it to you as to when we meet; do whatever is most convenient. There is no reason why I should not come to you for the first weekend.

We had a most amusing time on Sunday afternoon. I had arranged a shooting match against the Tramways Shooting Club for 4 o'clock. They arrived at the Provident Amt at 4 with a band and insisted on my team falling in with them and marching to the pub where we were going to shoot in the skittle alley. Fortunately I was in muftie [civilian clothes] and so escaped having to march. They were photographed and were in the papers. After a lot of beer we started to shoot, one at a time and didn't finish till 8.30. Then we had more beer and then speeches, which I had to translate and then I made one in my best German.

We were beaten at the shooting, but not by much. I have got quite a number of souvenirs, given to me by the football team, the shooting team etc, but as yet, no stamps.

The weather has turned to mild and sunny, really delightful. I went out to Homburg by car this morning to hand back some buildings vacated to the Government, a very nice trip through pretty country. No more now, I am busy working out details of transport etc.

Your loving son John

I have heard from York, he has not sold the car, and I also heard from Colonel Fisher, of Edinburgh fame congratulating me on my appointment!

John Rock
Polonnaruwa Rest House
Ceylon

Wednesday 5 February 1936
Evening

Dear Margaret,

I am writing this sitting on the rest house veranda by the light of the sun, which is just setting over the Kandy Hills in the West. The rest house is in a lovely position on the shores of a lake, with the Kandy Hills in the distance and jungle in the middle distance. I got here yesterday afternoon after driving the eighty miles from Trinco [Trincomalee], mostly in the rain, fifty miles back through the jungle towards Colombo and then thirty miles off to the left, still through jungle. It has luckily been fine ever since I have been here.

Polonnaruwa was one of the ancient capitals of the Sinhalese, which they built about 1100 AD after the Indian Tamils drove them out of Anuradhapura and they lived here for about two centuries till it in turn was captured by Tamils and the Sinhalese moved further south to Kandy. It was only discovered in the jungle about fifty years ago and is still being restored. The buildings are brick and stone and some of them, and the carvings, are very fine indeed. I went for a long walk through the jungle this morning, looking at the ruins and again this evening went round with a guide. This is the prettiest bit of jungle I've seen, with lots of very bright coloured birds, red and blue and yellow, but the only animal life I've seen are masses of grey monkeys and tortoises. I had to avoid running over the latter when I put my car away in the garage. Tomorrow morning, if your letters have arrived I shall leave here for Anuradhapura, about sixty or seventy miles north. If the mail hasn't come I may wait here another day for it.

They do [look after] one very well here, but I am dreading the bill. Dinner last night was Brown soup, fish out of the lake (which they called Lulu), simple roast on toast with rice and veg, roast chicken, egg custard and banana. I washed it down with lime juice.

The sun has just set and I'm going to have a bath. I have got the place all to myself. I took my last snap this morning and sent the negative off to Colombo to be developed.

The Rest House
Mullaitivu

Sunday (I think) 9 February 1936

This is one of the edges of beyond, it is just a fishing village on the N.E Coast, a collection of palm huts on long sand dunes by the sea. The only vegetation is Palmyra palms and cactus, and occasional ubiquitous coconut. The Rest House is brick, but is very primitive. I wonder what dinner tonight will be like? They have no beer in the place, blast them, and I needed some badly when I came in from a long walk, five or six miles along the sands by the sea.

There is a lovely stretch of sand by the sea and it made an excellent walk. The sands are covered with very pretty shells, the sort which used to fascinate us when we were children. At intervals along the coast were other fishing villages, mostly very smelly.

I left Anuradhapura this morning, after staying there two days and motored here along the Jaffna road to Maankulam, about fifty miles of straight and very good road through jungle, . I had lunch there at the rest house, quite a good rest house, fish omelette, sausages and mash and banana fritters and then I turned off the Jaffna road to here, thirty miles of very bad road through jungle. Tomorrow I shall go on to Jaffna about another ninety miles north. It is ever so much cooler and fresher and pleasanter here. There is a good N.E breeze. Polonnaruwa and Anuradhapura were both hot and moist and airless, typical jungle conditions.

I stayed at the Grand Hotel at A'pura [Anuradhapura]. An excellent hotel, extremely comfortable and very good food (Ceylon standards of course). Dinner my first night was hors d'oeuvre, fried fish, roast chicken, roast wild boar, blancmange, welsh rarebit, dessert and coffee. My meal tonight won't be that standard I'm afraid.

A'pura was only sixty miles from P'ruwa [Polonnaruwa], but except for a few Dagobas [small domed monument] they are very much ruins and it would take the expert eye of an archaeologist to find much interest in them. Anyway I got fed up with ruins, I suppose P'ruwa took the edge off my appetite for them. There were some pretty walks and drives though. The last evening there I motored about 8 miles to Michintale and climbed 1800 steps up a hill on which Buddha is supposed to have alighted on his first visit to Ceylon. There was a Dagoba and a very fine view from the top and various objects of interest on the way up, temples and such like. The whole of the end of one was filled by a huge reclining figure of Buddha and most of the body with figures of Buddhist monks squatting and listening to his words of wisdom, all were plastered and coloured and very ornate. Dravidian in origin. Most of the sculpture and building was done by Tamil slaves. A'pura dates back to 400BC.

Major Milne-Thompson and Captain Landers were both staying at the Grand Hotel, also a Mr and Mrs Calvert. The Calverts have four sons in the Corps, one senior to me and the rest junior.

Calvert had a job here and they are going home in April. Of the four sons, one is in India, one in Hong Kong, one in Singapore and one at Aldershot.

I'm afraid I shall have to go back to Trinco before Friday; my ready cash is running low and rest houses won't cash cheques and I could only cash one for R30/- at the Grand Hotel.

As an indication to Ma, I may say that the Grand Hotel at A'Pura cost R9 a day, i.e. 13/6, the Rest House at P'ruwa R8 a day i.e. 12/-. Fairly expensive. Those prices are exclusive of drinks.

I will leave this now till I get up to Jaffna. The car averaged 32.5 mpg over the first thousand miles. What does yours do , as a matter of interest? The tax is only R35/- and insurance R75/-.

Are you going to lay the Standard up when you come out here? If so, don't forget to have her greased all over, to have the battery taken out and charged every week and to have the car supported on the frame, so that the weight is taken off the wheels and springs.

If you are thinking of selling it I should think again, as you won't get anything for it and it will possess a considerable exchange value if and when you get another car.

P.S. I haven't had your last mail yet and shan't get it now till I get back to Trinco.

Rest House, Kankesanthurai

Tuesday 11 February, 5.30 pm

I'm afraid I have lost [missed] tomorrow's mail, so this will have to go Air Mail. I forgot the mail would close so much earlier here. This place is on the North Coast of Jaffna peninsula, about twelve miles North of Jaffna. I got here in time for lunch yesterday, about two o'clock having motored a hundred miles during the morning. This is about as far north as one can get. I am heading south again tomorrow. I shall probably make for Anuradhapura again, spend the night there and make Trinco in time for lunch on Thursday. All the first part of the journey yesterday was jungle, on a fair road, then the view broadened out to scrub, then sandy waste and the road got worse. On the Peninsula itself there is intense cultivation and masses of villages and the road is execrable. Jaffna I passed through on the way here and it is a fair sized town for Ceylon. The people up here are Tamils and are descendants of the original Tamil invaders of a thousand years ago or so. The rest house is clean and fairly comfortable. Far better than at Mullaitiva.

This morning I went for a long drive along the coast and over a causeway onto one of the islands and then over a ferry, which took an interminable time to another island and then about ten miles across the island to another ferry which should have taken me across to Jaffna and so home. But the last ferry was not running to I had to turn and come back again the same way.

It is typical of this country that a group of natives let me wait for the ferry for about ten minutes, when I asked one of them if it was Jaffna over there and he said, oh yes, it was Jaffna over there alright and added as an afterthought that the ferry was out of order.

Well, I really think that's all, so will close, with my best love to you and Mother.

From John

John Rock
Colombo

Monday 5 October 1936
7pm

Miss Rock
Windmill Hill
Near Hailsham
Sussex
England

Dear Margaret,

Yours and the Mater's letters arrived this weekend and also one of congratulations from Aunt Mabel. I am sending this Air Mail, as you will want to know a few details about the Eubank's bungalow.

They, leaving here the 7th, should reach you by the 17th. I expect last week's letters to Ma congratulating her on her umpteenth birthday was early.

Eubank now leaves end of November and Weld may arrive here end of December or may stay in Colombo to relieve Postle, who is taking the Staff College exam then, until middle of February; in which case you would get two months here, if you wanted it, and I would get very little leave.

There may be some difficulties about your getting the bungalow at all, but I think these can be overcome. Now Eubank is leaving:

> No cutlery or silver
> No linen
> Some crockery, details not yet decided.

1. I suggest you bring all the linen you need, sheets, table cloths, serviettes, dish-cloths etc and one

blanket each. I can lend you more if you get fever, which is the only occasion on which you need one above you.

2. I suggest you bring enough cutler and silver for a party of six, for on some occasion you will have to give one, I expect.

3. I suggest we buy any extra china or kitchen ware needed in Colombo, on the way here.

4. He is leaving all his furniture

5. I think you will still find using his bungalow cheaper than hiring an hotel or rest-house.

If you do have to live in the rest house, the sheets and towels will come in useful. They charge you R1/- each per day for sheets.

We played the Enterprise Marines at cricket on Thursday on the Big Maidan and beat them easily. I made 20 not out. Pretty good eh. We beat the Enterprise at hockey on Wednesday. So much for sport.

The M & C cricket team played Ceylon at Colombo on Saturday and half our sappers went over to see the match, so there were no games over the weekend.

T.P, Eubanks and I dined on board Enterprise last night. We were a select party and dined at a table on the upper deck. Afterwards we saw the flickers [movie]. I got up in the morning a little worse for wear and after spending most of the morning in the sun, it was really hot (I am sweating hard now). I had a slight temperature by lunch time. I am alright now, but shall take some quinine tonight.

I have a busy week before me, concreting tomorrow at the PWSS [Port War Signal Station], Wednesday at Nilaveli and Chapel Hill and Thursday, the roof of the last searchlight emplacement.

Hockey on Wednesday against Emerald, soccer on Saturday and cricket on Sunday.

We have three new additions to the barracks menagerie, a young hooded cobra, about a foot long, which was caught on the office steps and two baby wild hares, each about 3 inches long, which have to be fed milk with a spoon.

So much for tonight. Now for dinner (roast saddle of beef). It is a curious fact that, however hot it is, one still appreciates a hot meal.

No wonder Tony wouldn't retrieve. I trained him well and if he had stayed at Shornmead he might have been a respectable gun dog by now, but what with unlicensed chasing rabbits and seagulls and a ball and playing with his toy and the deleterious effect of female company, what can you expect of him. I think Colonel Wise showed great restraint in not shooting him (at Shornmead he never barked and retrieved fairly well, particularly duck.)

Tuesday 9.10pm

No more news so goodnight. Had a little practice at the nets tonight and then went to a cocktail party. I have to be at Nilaveli at 6.30 tomorrow morning.

Yours etc

John Rock

John was promoted to Captain on 3 September 1936. Tony was the family's much loved dog who must have spent time with John at Shornmead Fort in 1934. John was at Shornmead shortly before he was appointed Aide De Camp to the Commander in Charge of the International Force in the Saar Territory, Germany.

Margaret, Alice and Tony 1935

25 Dec 1936
R.A. Mess
Colombo

11am Christmas Day 1936

Dear Ma,

A merry Christmas to you once more. The day is warm and sunny and not much wind. I wonder what it is like at home now.

I fetched your parcel from the post office yesterday, so it couldn't have arrived more punctually.

Thank you very much indeed for the toilet case. I think it is an awfully good idea and will be very useful during my traveling about here. The box arrived intact and contained Margaret's, Connie's, Jeannie's presents and a Christmas cake. I suspect it was made by Margaret. Anyway, it was in beautiful condition and very rich. I nearly made myself ill by eating two slices for tea yesterday. I hope my parcel arrives in time for Christmas.

I had to have a dose of Eno's after tea before I was fit to dine out with Postlewaite. We went to the G.O.H and had a very good meal and sat on in the lounge till eleven watching the dancing and cabaret.

P.P. arrived on Wednesday morning. I went on board the trooper to meet him about eight o'clock and had a second breakfast on board. Who should I meet there but Mrs Care-Browne, wife of my ex C.O at Chatham who was on her way to Singapore to join her husband, who is Chief Engineer there. I took her and P.P. ashore and left her to go round the shops while I took P off to his quarters.

Then I went off round my office for an hour and then picked up Mrs C.B and P and we went to Mount Lavinia and had a bathe. There was quite a lot of surf and some big waves and poor Mrs C.B got knocked over once and scraped her face and shoulder on the sand. She isn't as young as she used to be, in fact she has a young son of nineteen. She is very straight-laced and proper, insisting on dressing and undressing in my car and left a large wet patch on the back seat. We then went on to the hotel and had lunch and I got back here in time to go on board again.

Unfortunately one of my Clerks of Works, who is a Warrant Officer celebrated the coming of the trooper by getting drunk and causing a disturbance in the Sergeants Mess that night and he is now under close arrest pending court martial. He is confined in a bunk in barracks and another W.O [Warrant Officer] has to stay with him day and night as escort, which is very bad luck for them over Christmas. P and I are relieving the escort during lunch today so that he can join his family for dinner.

It is causing us a lot of extra work, P has to prosecute and I defend him and altogether it's a foul nuisance.

I had Xmas Cards from Vance, Dorothy and Mrs Sheward and some from local people, but I think yours is the finest. Many thanks for the Stand magazine too.

Besides yours and M's letters I heard last mail from Uncle Herbert, who sent a cheque for £1 and from Jean, Connie and Jeannie and one or two people in India whom I met coming out.

I have had an invite from Hincks to visit him up-country in January and shall do so during my leave. I also wrote to the Hewetts in India who were so pressing that I should go and visit them. I had a reply from Mrs Hewett yesterday endorsing the invitation and asking me to join them on a hunting trip, but they are a little vague as to where they are going and whether they are going. It ought to be rather fun, if I can get the leave.

I have had lots of exercise lately. Squash Friday with Ashby and tennis on Saturday with P and squash again on Sunday and yesterday morning P and I went out to the garden club and played four sets there, doubles with two of the markers. We were the only people there. I slept soundly in the afternoon.

I have been spending the afternoons taking P round the garages. He wants something cheap and good which is very difficult to find and I am still looking for a light car to change mine for.

On Friday evening after dinner we went to Colonels Arndt's house (he is C.O of the C.E's) and all the C.E [Chief Engineers] officers were there and we played games, talked and drank. He has a particularly strong Dutch drink, old Brandy matured in a cask with raisins and apricots!

On Monday night we both dined with the Ellisons, so we have been having a gay time of it.

I will answer Margaret's letter next week, but please thank her from me for the sweater, it is awfully nice and fits beautifully. I can hardly believe she made it herself. The mail left at 6 this morning, so this will have to go by Air Mail.

What scandal about the Hincks! I must be careful what I repeat. I hope Tony will administer a thrashing to the Mahevly house's hound.

I'm so glad the sciatica is gone and do hope you don't get it again, The foam baths seem to have done it some good.

I'm afraid there is no chance of my getting a p.card to Philip by Jan!

I don't think there is any more news so goodbye now, my very best love to you both

    from John

I do hope you had a good Christmas.

John Rock
Colombo
Ceylon

19 July 1937

Mrs Rock
Windmill Hill
Nr Hailsham
Sussex
England

Dear Mater,

Yours and Margaret's letters arrived today, wishing me happy returns. Many thanks for them. I hope you will have got some people to stay with you by now and that you have had some summer to enjoy. The thought of strawberries makes my mouth water.

We went up to Kandy on Wednesday in three cars and a hired bus. We beat them at hockey that evening and drew with them at soccer next day, returning on Friday morning.

The troops had a very good time, but it ended in tragedy. Their bus crashed on the Trinco Road about five miles the other side of Habarana where the nearest hospital and doctor was.

Fortunately both Sgt. Andrews and my car were fairly close behind the bus and we arrived not long afterwards. There were twelve troops in the bus and a native driver and conductor. The driver was killed instantly and of the others, only two were uninjured. The bus itself was smashed to bits and its a miracle that any escaped.

There were no telephones of course and Andrews had to fetch the doctor from Dambulla, while I commandeered a bus in Habarana and fetched water etc.

They crashed about 12.15. It was two when the doctor arrived (he was out of course)and it was four before we got the last away to Dambulla and six before they got there.

This was on the 16th. Next morning we got the five worst cases off to Colombo by ambulance and the remainder yesterday. I stayed with two sappers to look after them and we returned yesterday in time for lunch.

Of the twelve sappers, five had serious fractures - leg, hip or pelvis, one broke his collar bone, one was badly cut and burnt, two were uninjured and the remainder various bruised, cut and shocked.

It was a terrible ending to a pleasant trip and a very grim experience. Only one motorist passed the whole time, going to Trinco, a native Trinco and two doctors and lots of cars arrived from there just as we were leaving the scene.

The Brigadier arrived today with the Colonel for his farewell inspection and I had the usual conducted tour. Tomorrow I shall be able to make up a week's arrears of work. I am still a little tired after Dambulla. There wasn't much sleep to be had there.

The weather here is still fine and warm and shows no sign of breaking. I apologise for the rather miserable letter.

Your loving son
John

John Rock
Colombo
Ceylon

Sunday 22 August 1937
10.55am

Dear Ma,

I'm afraid I missed the post again last week, so this goes by Air Mail. The list of troopers is out now. My relief, Churchill is almost sure to arrive on the Dorsetshire on Feb 28, and the next one back for me after that is the same ship returning. It leaves Colombo March 19 and arrives Southampton if punctual April 12. If I miss it, the next and last leaves here April 13 and gets home early in May.

The remainder of our bus crash cases are getting on very well. All the minor ones are back at work. There are still five in hospital. Some men are to be sent home, a man with a broken upper leg; and one with a burnt arm and cut face, who is subject to fits. The two dislocated hips and the broken lower leg are all pretty well now.

The gun is nearly finished now, and the gunners will probably go back to D'Wa next month. I have had some tummy trouble lately due to a chill after playing hockey against Enterprise on Sunday, but am myself again now.

We had a shooting match against Standford's crowd yesterday and just beat them. Our troops are improving. No more now, I will spread myself in a letter to Margareta tomorrow.

Your loving son

John

Margaret, Alice & John Rock 1930s

CHAPTER FOUR

The Road to France
1939 - 1940

Margaret and John's significant contribution to World War starts here.

Margaret and Alice moved to Cranleigh, Surrey and were soon called upon to take in evacuees leaving London. John was in Budapest in August 1939 and by 12 October 1939, he was in France.

By the time Britain declared war on Germany on 3 September 1939, work was already underway to get troops into France. The first wave of the British Expeditionary Force (B.E.F), commanded by General Lord Gort, started its journey in convoys to France in mid September 1939 and by 11 October 158,000 men had arrived without a single casualty. By March 1940 the B.E.F numbers in France had doubled.

The troops were mainly deployed in positions to defend the Franco - German border. This border was protected by the 'Maginot Line' made up of concrete fortifications, defended by French and British fighting forces. The Maginot Line ran from Switzerland to Luxembourg, with less robust fortifications running along the Belguim border to the English Channel, as neutral Belgium acted as a natural buffer between Germany and France.

On 10 May 1940 Germany carried out a glider and Blitzkreig (lightening war) attack. Within five days they had a strong foothold in Belguim, and after eighteen days of fighting, the Belgians surrendered.

Suddenly the Belgium buffer was at risk but British and French forces focused on the German troops facing them at the Maginot Line. The Allies advanced into Belgium unaware that German armoured units were advancing to the rear to cut them off from the remaining Allied force in France.

An aggressive German operation forced the British and French back toward the coast. With the ports of Calais and Bolougne occupied by the Germans on 26 May 1940, General Lord Gort ordered a retreat to the only viable evacuation point, Dunkirk.

It was feared that not all soldiers could be evacuated, but with assistance of 933 boats made up of Royal Navy vessels and approximately 700 fishing boats, pleasure crafts, lifeboats and merchant marine boats, over 300,000 British and French soldiers were evacuated by 3 June 1940.

In the lead up to May 1940 John's letter's offer a glimpse into the changing arena of war. He comments on the period of high alert in mid-November 1939, the German offensive in Norway, Gracie Fields entertaining troops in April 1940, and ultimately the end of the Phoney War - fighting had commenced.

John's letters stopped shortly after the attack on Belgium, but not before he had found out that Margaret had secured her new job. While John was fighting for his life, Margaret began her own wartime adventure at Bletchley Park.

Sunah
R.G Mess
Bordon

17 February 1939

The White House
Cranleigh
Surrey

Dear Margaret

Thank you for your open invitation and the congratulations. I should very much like to come over one Sunday. Life is very busy at the moment and I dislike making plans, so I don't expect I'll give you much warning.

Dunsfold is on the map but Cranleigh appears to be off the edge. However, with your lucid direction I should have no difficulty in finding it.

Glad you got your scarf back from the Mannlichen. I though the excellent Mr Stedham would not fail you! Of Harry I have not heard a word since we parted at Victoria station.

At the moment I am not feeling very influential as I am doing a substitute for a staff officer on Divisional Headquarters whilst he is on leave. So far the army still functions but I am hoping to produce such a laugh that manoeuvers have to be cancelled!

Yours Sunah

John Rock
Hotel Linza
Szolnok

8 August 1939

Miss Rock
The White House
Cranleigh
Surrey
England

I am back again after a quiet weekend in Budapest, where I had a good rest. It was too hot to do much, so I contented myself with a little sight-seeing. We had a grand day yesterday out at 5am and back at 8.30pm, and a very pleasant bathe. The reading is going well.

Love from John

John Rock
Hotel Tisza
Szolnok

11 August 1939

Ravenscourt
Hollincoundane Road
Ramsgate
Kent

Dear Ma,

Just a line to thank you for your letter and the wooly, both of which arrived here today. I got your first letter from the Legation, last weekend.

I have had a fairly busy and very pleasant week, and am not being worked anything like as hard now as when I first arrived. A curious thing, too, is that I find I can do with only three or four hours sleep at night and feel none the worse. I suppose it is a matter of getting used to it. I am still treated like a King, sometimes it is a little embarrassing. When I enter the Mess dining room, every one stands up. After dinner here, if we join a table to dance, I am always placed next to the prettiest girl, or between two of them. There are not many girls here, but they strike a very high standard.

You asked about the mess. It consists of a dining room and ante room and officers only lunch there, and sit about, if they have any spare time in the morning. They don't live there.

I mentioned my long jaunt on Monday in my PC to M. It was a lovely day, fine and sunny, but not too hot. We rode out with the battalion about 18km, stopping to watch their exercises occasionally. The country is very pastoral, almost mediaevally so. There are even goose girls and large flocks of geese. We reached the river about

10am, having left at five and we stayed there till four in the evening, bathing, eating and dozing. There was a basket maker there, making baskets by the reed beds and I watched him for a long time.

On Tuesday, I attended a shooting match of the officers in the garrison, pistol and rifle, and there were twelve good prices for each. We shot the pistol first and to my horror I won it. I was terrified of winning the rifle too, but came nowhere near it, thank goodness.

However, I got a cigarette case and a plaque as prizes. That night we celebrated my victory. After dancing here till 12, we went to another cafe, where they have a ligana band and sat there till 3.30. They have a bad habit of what they call drinking to X. It means emptying ones glass at one gulp. I had to be up by 7 next morning and felt few ill effects. That morning I was taken to the flying ground and shown all their gliders and how pupils are trained. I was also given a free trip over Szolnok in an aeroplane.

In the afternoon, we saw a demonstration of gliding. Very good indeed. A pilot in a glider was towed up 3000 feet by an aeroplane and there released. He did every possible stunt on the way down, including flying on his back.

Today we went off by car to visit another one about 80 km away and got back this evening.

Tomorrow, I mount at seven and ride out to see some shooting. I find I have said little about recreation. I have bathed once or twice and played bridge once, at the club.

The food is peculiar, but excellent. The wine unexceptionable and beer a good deal better than German.

Thanks for the address in France. I can not inform all concerned.

I do hope both you and Margareta have fine weather for your holidays. I seem to be having the best of it. It has been a little cooler the last day or so.

I can now count up to a hundred in Hungarian, rather shakily, and that is about all I have learnt.

Love from John

John Rock
Hotel Tisza
Szolnok

15 August 1939

Mrs Rock
Lyndhurst
Beach Road
Littlehampton
Sussex

Dear Mother

I received two letters from you this morning, one dated 13th and one forwarded by the Legation, dated 5th. I gathered one had gone astray.

First as to my address. I stay in Szolnok till the 19th, when I go to Budapest. I don't know yet which hotel I shall stay in there, but the Legation address will find me. I shall probably leave Budapest for Munchen on the morning of the 23rd. I have written to Fran G. asking her to recommend me a hotel in Munich, but have so far had no answer. I will let you, as soon as I find out myself. I shall probably stay there till 29th or 30th when I shall go on to Irguy, it depends on the times of the trains.

I do hope the weather has improved for yous and Margaret's holidays and that it will be warm in France, you appear to have had an awful wet, cold time.

I had a very pleasant day on Sunday. I spent the week-end in Szolnok, and was invited to go to Church (RC) with the troops in the morning. The service was at 8, so I had to get up at 6.30. After walking back, I changed and went over to the club, with one of the officers. There I spent the whole day in a bathing dress, it being warm and sunny. I started by going for row, in a four. We went up stream about 2 and 1/2 miles, landed at a pub for a drink of beer and then rowed back with the stream.

I then bathed and sub-bathed till lunch-time. The river flows so fast that one can only just swim against it, it is about 150 yards wide. The pleasant way of bathing is to walk two or three hundred yards up stream and then come down with the stream.

I lunched at the club, dozed after lunch, bathed and sun-bathed again till about 6, and then played bridge till it was time to return here for dinner. I went to bed early (11pm) pretty tired and sleepy.

Yesterday, I had quite a light mornings work and in the evening went to a big dinner at the Mess, which all the officers and their wives attended. As usual it involved drinking much more than I like to. I spent the evening dancing and had really a most enjoyable time, getting to bed soon after four. Thank God, today is a public holiday, and I was able to stay in bed till eleven this morning. It is now getting on for lunchtime; I shall probably sleep again after lunch and go to the club for a bathe in the evening.

Everyone here is extraordinarily kind and hospitable and it distresses me that I have absolutely no opportunity of returning their hospitality.

My first day or two in Budapest is going to be pretty full. An officer is coming up with me on Saturday to show one of the sights. That will mean a pretty late night, I expect.

Sunday is St Stephens Day, the big Hungarian national fete day, and I have been given a pass to see the procession from the War Office. It ought to be most interesting, but as I have to be there in uniform at 7.45 am, I doubt if I shall get to bed at all. I shall probably finish the night at a Turkish bath and then go and get changed. I doubt if I shall do much more sight-seeing on Sunday, but I have Monday and Tuesday to have a look round.

I will now close, and will write to you again from Budapest on Sunday or Monday, earlier if I get an address in Munich from Fran G.

My best love
John Rock

John Rock
Park Hotel
Budapest

Monday morning 21 August 1939

Lyndhurst
Beach Road
Littlehampton

Dear Mother,

Here I am back in Budapest again, and my attachment is over. It was hard work at times, but extremely interesting and pleasant and I would not have missed it for anything. Most of the infantry officers went off for an exercise on Wednesday and I said goodbye to them then. On Thursday I had a late morning and a quiet day, and on Friday I spent the whole day out with three of the officers shooting partridges. We did it in style, going out by car and having an excellent lunch sent out in a cart. The shooting was good, but I let the side down by shooting very badly. One walked across heavy plough, between the rows of head-high maize, through which the beaters stumbled. Melons grew in the maize strips as well. Every now and and then a bird would get up out of the maize. We all turned in early on Friday night.

On Saturday morning I packed and went in uniform to the barracks for lunch, where we had a farewell speech or two, and then they all escorted me to the station and saw me off by the 2.20. I presented them with a copy of our Corps History in Egypt and the Sudan and received a flask of Barrack scnapps.

A sapper officer came up with me and I first came here and settled in and got my uniform ready for the morning. I had changed back into mufti at the barracks before leaving.

We then went out to the Gellert Hotel, the one with all the swimming baths, for six o'clock coffee, and on from there to restaurant for supper at eight. We then came back here again and I got into a dinner jcket and off we went again to the Margareteu lusel [Margaret Island], a long narrow island in the middle of the Donau [Danube River]. It was too early for a night club, so we had another coffee in a restaurant and on from there to the Parisienne, a very fun 'lokal', where we had a box and stayed till 3.15, drinking, dancing and watching the cabaret. I returned at 3.15 to get some sleep leaving him there.

I was up at six on the Sunday and went off, feeling completely fresh, to the War Office to see the procession, Sunday being St Stephens Day, Hungary's greatest national Holiday. It was really a religious procession but the uniforms and vestments were magnificent. A crowd of peasants all in the most beautiful national costumes followed it. I waited to see it return, about 11 am, beginning then to feel a bit sleepy, and then went off with Barclay to their [equivalent of] Sandhurst, to see the passing out ceremony of their cadets.

All the military Attachés were there and I have seldom seen so many different uniforms. Barclay outshone them all, with full dress of the Black Watch. We had a drink afterwards I came back for lunch and bed.

The town yesterday was crammed full of people up from the country. After dinner, we could hardly move in the streets.

The last week it has rained a good deal and been quite cool, now it is a good deal warmer, but nothing like when I was first here.

I have not heard from Sigrid, but shall probably get an address of a hotel in Munich from Barclay this morning.

That is all I think. I leave by the 10 am train on Wednesday reaching Munich about 10 pm.

My love and auf w [auf weidersehen]

John Rock L; C LP1 RDF

Saturday 7.15pm

As you see, I'm back in Budapest again, having come up for the weekend to see the lights, and shall go out and have dinner after finishing this letter. Tomorrow morning I shall be visiting Barclay some time I suspect, he is ringing me at nine and I have been recommended a hotel where one can bathe all the morning and lunch afterwards.

In fact, when I announced I was coming here for the weekend, a small committee of officers sat and arranged a complete programme for me, with the numbers of every bus I had to take and wrote it out for me. Needless to say, I shall not follow it, though I shall have to give a strict account of my adventures.

As to the climate, it is very hot indeed. I am sweating now, at this time of the evening. Szolnok is colder than Buda, but baking between nine and six.

The country is so flat as an unsuccessful souffle and entirely agricultural, mostly maize. There are quite a lot of trees and hedges scattered about and it is quite pleasant to look at. The villages are clean and bright.

My hotel at Szolnok is really quite good, large aviary and with a big terrace facing the river Linza. We take all our meals outdoors on the terrace, except lunch, which all the officers eat together in barracks. This is their main meal of the day.

Now a little to my life there. I am treated extraordinarily well. They go out of their way to be friendly and to make one feel at home. On the other hand I have to keep to their working hours and they start early and work til one.

When I finished my last letter, I was about to go for my first ride. That was hell, neither more nor less. We started at seven and go back at ten, the colonel, another officer, my bear leader and I and a train of attendant orderlies. I did everything but fall off and might really have never been on a horse before. When we got back it was blazing hot and I was throughly exhausted and soaked to the skin. However, I went riding again this morning and we had a much easier time. My muscles are coming back and I feel quite reasonably at home.

On Monday we have to be mounted at 5am, having breakfasted and are off with the battalion for a days training. We lunch out and take bathing dresses and towels. It ought to be quite amusing. I am returning by eight pm tomorrow in order to get a nights sleep.

After the mornings work we usually lunch in the mess at 1.30 and I get back to my pub, about 1/2 hours away, by 3. Then I change into pyjamas, clean my buttons for the next day and turn in.

At six I join the other unmarried officers at a cafe, where they have their own table for coffee. Than we go for a short stroll along the river and so back to the pub. I change from uniform into mess and join them for dinner on the terrace of the hotel Linza, where again they have their own table and we sit and talk and drink and dance till I retire about midnight. Quite a good life but it takes a little getting used to.

A very nice fellow indeed has been told to look after me and he does his job remarkably well. In fact the only thing I can complain of is that I am never alone at all, and that is rather an ungrateful thing to say.

For instance, he provided a carriage to take me to the station, saw me off himself, has arranged for the carriage to meet me again and regretted that he was unable to accompany me here, as he is moving his furniture into a new house tomorrow.

I have no difficulty in the language question, as I can talk German as well as most of them and better than several. Quite a few talk only Hungarian. Now I must be off to dinner

Best love from John
No letter from you yet.

John Rock
3.T.B.R.E
Gordon Barracks
Ripon

Tuesday 19 September 1939

The White House
Cranleigh

Dear Margarita

I hope you are not still being overworked and that your evacuees are settling down. Please thank Mother for her letters and for the serviette ring. I haven't had the letter she sent to the War Office, I doubt if it ever arrives. I hear now that such letters should be addressed 'Army Post Office'.

I have been up here ten days or so now, but it does not seem so long. I have not had a great deal of work to do, engaging and administering civilians and shall be given the Officers Mess to run again soon, I expect.

I am getting plenty of practice at darts. We have a board in the mess and it is used a lot. We had a match against the local police the other night and beat them. I succeeded in what is known as 'whitewashing' my opponent; that is winning out before he gets his first double.

I took my car to Leeds yesterday and spent all day at the Labour Exchange there, engaging waiters and batmen for the mess. I lunched in the town and came back in the evening. It is quite a pretty run through Harrogate, about thirty-five miles. Leeds is a large town but quite pleasant one, with very good shops and excellent roads.

I went off in plain clothes on Sunday morning, first of all to the Fountain Abbey, which is quite close, but it was shut up on Sunday and then up to the moors, also not far away. They are very dark and forbidding. I left the car and went for a longish walk and had lunch at a pub and then back to sleep it off.

I enjoy listening to the Yorkshire dialect, I had never heard thee and thou used before.

Poor Poland seems to be out of it now, and it looks as if we should both settle down seriously to siege warfare. I think it is only a matter of time before Italy and the USA come in with us, I hope so anyway, but I have a nasty feeling that Hungary and Bulgaria are going to march into Rumania. I wonder what side Turkey will join, if either? These are all idle speculations. I also wonder where our army is now.

Give my love to Mother. I hope she is not taking the raids too seriously now and that Nancy is getting enough sleep.

Yours John Rock

It is pretty chilly up here and no fires yet, but I am getting my hot bath now.

A Batman in the British military was a regular solider or airman appointed as the personal servant of a commissioned officer.

John Rock
No 2 Military Mission
C/O Station Commandant R.A.F
Hendon
The Hyde N.W.9

12 October 1939

The White House
Cranleigh

Dear Mother,

This is to wish you many happy returns of the day and I do hope it arrives in time. It will not leave till tomorrow evenings post, and should arrive alright, unless the weather is bad. I left Margaret some cash, and she promised to get me a small gift for you. I am only sorry I cannot send one myself.

I have now had two letters from you, and one from Margaret, many thanks for them. I received the cheque and drafts and am sending them straight to the bank.

I will drop a note to Ripon and ask them for my tankard again.

I should think I am very likely to come home like Alec. I have an excellent appetite and gorge myself on the good food, and I only get an hour or so exercise about every other day. I am starting at the beginning of the wine list and working my way through it. I had a very good Aryan this evening. They are mostly about 16-20 francs a bottle, and the dinner costs 18 francs, also lunch. Tomorrow we are giving a slap-up lunch party to our friends. I helped chose the menu with my host, and I am sure I shall not be able to do any work afterwards. We are repeating a particularly fine souffle which we had the other day.

Thank you so much for the offer of a paper. I should

be awfully grateful for Punch. We get the Times every evening of the same day it is issued. Better off, in fact, than Paris or Scotland.

We have had one or two very wet days lately, but generally it is fine and we get a good deal of sun. The garden paths are carpeted with chestnuts, how I should have loved it as a child.

I went off yesterday with Lynfield and Fonseka in the latter's car in the afternoon, up the hill and into the country, and went for a walk. The woods are looking lovely and the trees just beginning to change colour.

I have no more news for the present, so will close with much love to you both.

John Rock

I will send you congratulations should the occasion arise. It certainly has not done so yet.

John Rock
No 2 Mission
c/o Registry
Air Ministry
King Charles Street
Whitehall S.W.1

France 24 October 1939
(By A.D.L.S. Bag D)

The White House
Cranleigh

Dear Margaret

I don't believe I have ever replied to your kind letter. I have now been in the country three weeks, and it seems a good bit longer. Nothing has happened to disturb the even tenor of our lives and nothing seems likely to. I have seldom known a situation of more uncertainty.

The notice of our change of address came in yesterday evening, just before the mail left, so I scribbled off a line to Mother at once, to let you know. Anything in the mail with the previous address on it will probably reach me alright.

We are lucky here, compared with our compatriots elsewhere, who I hear are living under very different conditions.

Winter is drawing in, but very slowly, yesterday was sunny and quite hot. Today, by contrast, is cold and drizzly.

I went out for a very pleasant drive, the other day on business, through a lot of woodland. The trees are just beginning to turn yellow and the woods on the slopes round here are beautiful.

Bolster has been away for three days, and I have been doing his work as well, and found my time pretty full. He is now back, and today seems idle by comparison.

Lynfield has taken to eating a sandwich lunch in his office, midday, with the object of reducing perhaps, so I have lunch by myself now, but all three of us normally dine together, and there are often visitors as well, sometimes distinguished ones.

The Garde Mobile on our gate has adopted a dog, a mongrel Alsatian, who is very reminiscent of Jumbo, he is young and very friendly.

I wonder how the Villa boys are employed now. Mrs Villa must be having an anxious time.

I heard from Ripon the other day; they have not had their mess bills either, so I don't think Mother need expect mine for some time.

From Mother's letters, she is getting a little fed up with the evacuees. God help you if you had had some of the brats I've seen in Cranleigh. Having one's flowers dug up is a small price for being bugless. I continue to wax fat on good food. We had an oyster lunch the other day.

Au revoir

John Rock

GRAND QUARTIER GÉNÉRAL DES ARMÉES

Carte d'Identité N°

délivrée à

Le Général, Major Général des Armées :

NOTA. — Voir au dos une observation importante.

BRITISH EXPEDITIONARY FORCE

ARMÉE   BRITANNIQUE

Duty Order—
    Serving as Temporary Travel Permit outside the Zone of the British Army and L. of C. as defined from time to time.

Order de Mission—
    Servant de Titre de Circulation Temporaire pour se rendre en dehors de la Zone de l'Armée Britannique et de ses Lignes de Communications telles qu'elles seront définies en temps opportun.

No. of Bearer's Identity Card	No. of Motor Car
No. de la Carte d'Identité du Titulaire 717	No. de l'Automobile
Rank / Grade CAPTAIN	Name / Nom J.F. ROOK
Unit or Appointment / Corps au Service ROYAL ENGINEERS	
Proceeding from / Se rendant de LA FERTÉ-SOUS-	To / À LONDRES
Itinéraire / Route PAR LA VOIE DES AIRES	
Nature of Duty / Mission MISSION SPECIALE	
Validity from / Validité de Le 5 Mars	To / À 7 Mars. 1940

Signature, Rank and Appointment of Issuing Officer
Signature, Grade et Service de l'Officier Émetteur   Lieut-Colonel.

Stamp of Issuing Office
Cachet du Service Émetteur

Signature of Recipient.
Signature du Titulaire.

Stamp of P.M. when Duty order exceeds one duty or journey

John Rock in France 1939 - 1940

John Rock
France

Saturday 4 November 1939

The White House
Cranleigh

Dear Margarita

Just a line in reply to your charming letter of Nov 2, which I was very pleased to get. Please thank Mother for the Punch which arrived along with it.

There was not sign, however, of the 1/2 of Bondman which I asked Mother for in my last letter. I wonder if you would send it off when you get this, if you have not done so already, as I am getting short and a little anxious.

The weather is warm and damp, a good deal of rain, but a lovely day yesterday. No time for more.

Love from John

John Rock
France

14 November 1939

The White House
Cranleigh

My dear Margaret

I enclose a cheque for £25, being the second instalment of your yearly allowance. I'm sorry that it is so late.

I have now a little leisure again, after several busy days, but that does not mean that the danger of the balloon going up is not the same as before. Personally I think it is still likely.

Tomorrow I am going up to what can only be described as a neighbouring large town, to buy some pyjamas, two of my pairs not having stood up to the washing line.

I should be grateful if you would send me out four sets of darts, of the size and weight you use (brass ones) as our initial issue were not of good quality (charge to my account). Also I asked Mother to let me have 1/2 of Bondman weekly for the next month, could you ask her to send eight one ounce tins, as I haven't got a tobacco jar here.

I hope you noted the remarks about the treatment of my car in my last letter to Mother.

I leave to you as to whether you license it. I should hardly think it will be worth your while, but if you like, lay yours up and use mine. Anyhow, I don't think I would see mine for another year at least, unless you are offered a very good price.

The weather has been extraordinarily mild for the time of year and alternately wet and sunny.

Now it is a little colder and apt to be misty. I went out

for half an hours stroll this morning and am going for another when I have finished this.

By the way, I shall be home, I hope, on leave on Feb 7, returning on Feb 18, and going both ways by air. That is, if nothing untoward happens in the interval.

My love to Mother

Yours John Rock

In early October Hitler had informed his commanders of his plans to commence an attack through Holland, Belgium and France on 14 November 1939. A leak by German officers ensured the British Government knew of the date and the forces in France were on high alert. Hitler cancelled the plans on 10 November to allow his army more time to prepare.

John Rock
France

Saturday 9 December 1939

The White House
Cranleigh

Dear Margaret

Many thanks for your letter, and for the mittens, it was very kind indeed of you to think of making them for me.

Did you like my postcard? They are a great boon to lazy letter-writers and I shall make full use of them.

Mothers tobacco arrived safely yesterday. I now have a good reserve of stock of it.

The weather has been very changeable. We had it fairly cold for a few days, and now it has turned warm and muggy again. I would very much rather it has stayed cold, it isn't like December at all, except for the rain.

We have had lots of visitors lately, of all ranks and both nationalities. The King did not visit us, but the Brigadier went and had dinner with him and returned very pleased with himself, being sat between the King and the Duke of Gloucester.

Life is generally very quiet, the alarms and excursions of 12-15 November and the month before that have not been repeated, but you may see an interesting piece of news in the paper on the 11th.

I still go for my walks whenever I can, but the countryside is very bleak now. Lynfield, who is still a subaltern at 39, has been trying very hard to get himself promoted Captain, and is very sore because G.H.Q have turned it down. Fonseca's leg is a little better, but being more French than most Frenchman and being a nervous and restless temperament he hates having to sit still. The

Brigadier's lumbago is alright again and I have enjoyed uniformly good health.

Thank you very much for the pullover, I will expect it after Christmas and please don't hurry yourself, as you must be very busy.

No I don't think you need worry about making me socks or a helmet, you see, we live here in the greatest luxury and comfort. I am often ashamed of it. We live on the fat of the land at the Hotel de L'Epee and are the envy of the officers from G.H.Q who visit us.

I am just going out for a visit to one of the Bureaux, so will close, with love to all, not forgetting Tony

Yours John Rock

P.S After finishing the one book I have read here, I have not been able to start another. My office is also my living-room and as soon as I start to read, the telephone rings or someone calls or a letter arrives. However, I am waxing fat on it.

John Rock
Somewhere in France

22 December 1939

The White House
Cranleigh

Dear Margaret

This is the first of all to wish you a Merry Christmas and very happy New year and secondly to thank you very much for your parcel. It arrived safely yesterday. The woolly is awfully well made and fits beautifully and is very comfortable this weather. It has been freezing hard the last few days, but has been fine and clear and sunny. I am sorry for the troops up the line.

Your cake looks delicious and arrived in good order. As Bolster had had one from his sister two days before, we are keeping yours until his is finished. The pudding we shall eat at the Epee on Christmas Day.

I also got your letter and Mrs Foot's this evening. She says Mother is a very fine woman. Hear! Hear!

Yes please do write to my insurance co and ask for the money back, if any. I hope you made a note of the instruction for buying the car.

I hope the stockings arrived safely. I hear the customs did not look at them. If they are a wrong shade or size, please do return them with your full instruction and I will change them. I walked in, bold as brass, into a shop hung with corsets and things to get them. I had a look at the girls' foot who was serving me, and it seemed about your size, so I asked for some the same size as hers.

It has just occurred to me that I have forgotten to send Nancy anything and I will try to get something small tomorrow. But I can't remember her surname. Is it Nott or Jones, or something else. I fancy it is something else, so will address it to you.

I'm sorry she has been indisposed. Will you remind Mother to send me Aunt Florence's address.

My best love

John Rock

John Rock
France

27 Jan 1940

The White House
Cranleigh

Dear Margaret

I can now give you the firm dates of my leave, if all goes well. I leave here on Feb 7 and should arrive in London about 4 pm of that day, if the plane is not late. If the weather is bad and the plane does not fly, I travel by boat and get in I expect that night or next morning. In the first case, that of my flying, I might go to a shop or two while in London and come down by train, getting in for a late supper. In any case, I will phone you from Guildford and if you are out take a taxi in.

I leave on 18th. I am afraid the details are a bit vague. If you like, I will ring you up from London and arrange what train I shall come by. Let me know if you would like me to do that and if so, will you be prepared with a list of trains.

The great frost has broken at last here. We must have had three weeks of it, with snow on the ground all the time and the river frozen bank to bank.

It broke yesterday afternoon when it started to rain and is still raining. Unfortunately, the ground is only just beginning to thaw, 24 hours later. So, as the rain fell, it froze solid on the roads, paths and steps. This morning there was about 1/2 inch of ice over everything. All road transport has been at a standstill now for 24 hours and only the younger and more agile pedestrian could get along. I walked down to the Epee last night with Bolster, who is back from his skiing leave. He had no nails in his boots and when he got to the gutter, I had to take his hand and pull him up the camber.

We were lucky and got away with only one burst pipe, but it did a good deal of damage. It was in Lynfield's bedroom on the second floor and he is on leave. It soaked down into the guest-room on the first floor, which was unoccupied and it wasn't till it reached our office on the ground floor, that we noticed it.

I am glad you have had some skating and I wish I could have got some. There was plenty of ice about and the ice on the river hasn't broken in spite of the rain.

Poor Nancy, she must have had a cold journey. I hope her train was not snowed up, a great many here were. I think the day I went up to Paris was one of the coldest we had and I certainly never intended to take her to Versailles. Even the cinema I went to wasn't hot.

My love to Mother

Yours John Rock

John Rock
France

25 March 1940

The White House
Cranleigh

Dear Margaret

Many thanks for your letter of the 15th. It is quite springlike here now. The chestnuts are just coming out in leaf and the woods full of anemones and violets. I have even seen a cowslip.

The weather is warm and muggy. My relief arrives on Wednesday afternoon and I leave here on Saturday morning for my new abode. My new address I will repeat, it is:

HQ 13 Infantry Brigade, B.E.F

I shall be sorry in many ways to leave a job and people I know well and to have to start again on an entirely different job among strangers, but on the other hand, it is what I wanted and the change will be very pleasant. It will be much more active, open air life and I need that badly. I should have hated to have spent the summer here.

I hope you will hear about a job soon. I mentioned it to Pritchard and he said he would remind his chief, who is coming over in a few days. Their department is notoriously casual and hardly organised.

I expect there is plenty to do in the garden. Mother's letter has just arrived. I see they have sent you an application form. I expect the affair will déroule [unravel] slowly.

Mother says you had an unpleasantness with the Bundys over the husband coming for Easter. A few more like that and she may go of her own accord. I do hope she will go before you do.

I note Mother has lost a stone, while I have been gaining steadily. I expect it is all the hard work she has been putting in. You will have to feed her on Cod Liver Oil. I met an officer at G.H.Q who had been one of my instructors at Camberley and he remarked on how fat I was getting. I shall be able to live on it in my next job.

I enclose half-yearly cheque.

Yours affectionately

John Rock

John Rock
HQ 13
Infantry Brigade
B.E.F

30 March 1940

The White House
Cranleigh

Dear Mother

Just a line to let know I have arrived here safely. De Fonseka very kindly motored me over in his 33 HP Cadillac, a monster of a car and rather draughty.

It was a rotten day and rained most of the way. We left at half-past nine and got in here about 3 o'clock, lunching at a place I have already visited several times.

To my surprise I find we are even more comfortably installed than we were in my last place. Our offices occupy one large private home and our mess another about a hundred yards distant. I have just dined there, quite well, though not up to the Tratchet's standard and have returned to the office to write to you. I sleep alone here tonight and for a week and then take over a luxurious billet near the mess.

Fonseca only stayed long enough to meet the Brigadier and have my luggage unloaded and then pushed off, to get as far as possible back in daylight.

I was given a very good send off. We all dined together at the Epee last night. (I was deputed to choose the meal and wine) and I was seen off by the Mission this morning, except the Brigadier, who is in bed, I am afraid with the German measles.

Anyway, they were all very kind to me indeed and in many ways I regret leaving.

The chap I am replacing has already left. We are in for a weeks considerable activity, in which I have to perform my main job and then my predecessor returns for a few days to hand over.

So I am afraid you will not hear from me again for a week. I have already ploughed into work and am so sleepy I shall so go straight to bed now.

I think my period of leave is going to be advanced to May, probably to the latter end, as a result of coming here. How does that affect you?

With all my love

John Rock

Herbert Simmonds
Lynlow
Parkfield Avenue
Amersham Common
Bucks

8 April 1940

The White House
Cranleigh

My dearest Margaret

Just a few lines to congratulate you on getting a war job if I may call it that. I am not asking what it is and wonder if it is a paid or unpaid job. I am very pleased to know you may be in our neighbourhood, if you are please come and look us up whenever it is possible. May I also add that whenever you want a rest please make use of our house, it may happen that it would be further for you to go home than come here so please come here.

The weather is awful just now and icy cold. My throat is still bad. I went out this morning, the wind was very keen so I hope I have not made my throat any worse.

Please thank your mother for her last letter. I will answer it later. I hope John did not catch the German Measles. Your mother will not like being alone so I wonder what she will do. Poor Tony will miss you very much. I wonder if the evacs are leaving you.

Tuesday 9 April

The news from Norway is great I have just listened to a special broadcast at 10.30 confirming the news that Germany has invaded Norway and Denmark and have occupied and bombed places in those countries so now we may expect to hear what we are going to do in this matter. Auntie sends her love and says there will always be a bed for you whenever you can avail yourself of it.

I hope to have a little walk with Jackie but the wind is still very keen. Our love to your Mother and yourself.

Your affectionately

Herbert S Simmonds

Herbert *Simmonds is Alice Rock's younger brother. The family visited Herbert and his wife at their home in Amersham, Buckinghamshire. This gave Margaret the reassurance of a close relative nearby to her new job at Bletchley Park.*

John Rock
B.E.F

9 April 1940

The White House
Cranleigh

Dear Margaret

I am so glad to hear you have got the job at last and I hope you will like it. I expect you will become an expert in no time.

I see you start on the 15th. This is short notice to get rid of the Bundy's and I hope you succeed in doing so.

What a good thing you are close to Herbert and Jean. It will give you somewhere to go in your off-time, if you have any. I expect you will take the car. You might have another look at mine before you go and see that the battery has been taken out. You have never said if they have mended my radiator.

My congratulations to Norah on reaching commissioned rank. I shall look forward to seeing her in uniform.

I wonder if you would send me one of the films out of my zinc lined case. It is labeled Staff Duties or perhaps S.D and is a fat one.

I doubt now if I shall be going on leave before the end of June or early July, as I have to wait till my Brigadier has come back from his and I think he is putting it off.

The weather is none too good. Cold winds, rain and very little sun. It is much more bracing up here and my appetite is better, though the fare is not so good.

I have a awful lot to learn about this job. I [am] always fated to start something quite new, each time I move.

There is plenty of news on the wireless just now. I wonder what will come of it all.

Love to Mother
From John Rock

Sir Arthur Durston
Clapgate
Latton Common
Harlow
Essex

12 April 1940

Miss Rock
The White House
Cranleigh
Surrey

My dear Margaret,

So glad to see by your letter received this afternoon that you had been given the appointment you had applied for. Many thanks for writing, it was a great pleasure to write on your behalf and I hope it helped towards clinching the matter. Anyhow it did no harm, obviously.

So glad to know that mother is being relieved of the evacuees for you have had your full share of them and more than done your bit.

When Ruth and Martha return to school next Wednesday we shall be indeed quiet as the two teachers who were billeted with us have gone home. The one who was with us for a month had then joined her hubby in the Village always looked on our cottage as her home here and was always popping in. It was great comfort for Con and whenever I had any meetings she always used to come round and keep Con company.

Yes, I am quite fit again, thank you. Got back into routine last Sunday for light duty and commence full duty on Monday. Weather has not been too congenial for gardening and A.R.P. had kept me busy with inspection of gas masks and first aid lectures. Traffic control and H.E.

and Incendiary bombs, to say nothing of exercises.

Hope you will like your new job and here's wishing you the best of luck in it from us all.

Our best love to you and mother and to trust you are both well.

Yours affectionately

A.S.W.Durston

Arthur Sidney Wilkinson Durston, Captain Royal Navy. Friend of Margaret's father, Frank Ernest Rock and the father in law of Ernest's brother, Herbert Rock.

Margaret's 'appointment' was her new job at Bletchley Park, the Government Code & Cipher School's code breaking operation in the Buckinghamshire countryside.

John Rock
BEF

25 April 1940

The White House
Cranleigh

Dear Mother

After three really warm sunny summer days it has started to pour with rain again and has turned beastly cold. I wish the summer would make up its mind to come and stay a little.

I enclose a list of the kit which I left behind at the mission, together with a couple of suitcases. I have asked Lynfield to get it sent home. It may be sent direct to you or it may be left in London to be collected. If the latter happens I will let you know where it is and perhaps you would fetch it home on your next visit.

I have also posted you a small parcel from here containing an old holster and field-glasses case. We have web equipment which carries things like that now.

We have a tennis court at the back of our chateau and I have played on three evenings lately. It made me a bit stiff, but the exercise did me a world of good.

I get out of the office very little indeed at the moment, partly because I am not au fait and it takes me longer than necessary to do things, but I am nothing like as hard-worked as I was for the first month or so in my last job, where I only lived from meal to meal.

I am very glad to hear the Bundy family has left. They must have been an awful load off your mind. Fancy them pinching your flowers!

Did I tell you I had been into a large town near here for dinner about three nights ago with the Brig[adier] and two others, and after dinner we went to the theatre and saw a British variety show, given for the troops.

It was a huge theatre, about the size of the Princes, and crammed to capacity with men. The performance was first rate. Jack Hylton's band was on the stage most of the time and Gracie Fields entertained at the piano half the evening. She was very good indeed and the troops loved it. The dinner was excellent but very expensive. The shop-keepers and restaurants in this area think they can make their fortunes out of the B.E.F.

Time passes quickly. I never seem to know what day it is. I have been here nearly a month now. It doesn't seem so long.

The news from Norway has been good. I think we have the Germans just where we want them there. It was a very great mistake on their part.

I have thrown off my cold now and will hope not to get any more for a bit.

Please let me have Margaret's address if you know it.

Your loving son John

I got the cheque alright and I fancy a Punch or two since I last wrote.

Germany launched a surprise attack on Norway on the night of 8-9 April 1940. British and French troops were deployed on 14 April 1940, but landed amid swelling German troops. The campaign was lost and the British and French troops evacuated 6 weeks later.

John Rock
B.E.F

Thursday 9 May 1940

The White House
Cranleigh

Dear Mother

My Brigadier has gone on leave and is due back on the 18th. I am due to go myself on the 20th as ever is, as soon in fact as he gets back.

It may be inconvenient and it may mean not getting leave at the same time as Margaret, but as so many things may happen to stop one getting leave later, it is a sound principle to take it when one can. If nothing intervenes, therefore, I shall be home on the 20th or 21st May.

Would you please ask Margaret to get my car fully insured from 20th to 5th June.

The weather is still gorgeous and the country beautiful. We lead an idyllic life. I went for a walk this afternoon through a large wood. It was carperted with bluebells, and cowslips are still out in profusion.

I went into a large town, some distance away, yesterday, with our French liaison officer, who this time is a young second lieutenant and took tea with the owner of our chateau, the Contesse de Guyencourt. She had quite a large party of her own nationality there and I had a little more practice with the language.

I think of going over to the Mission on Saturday, to stay for the night and come back Sunday evening. It is about seventy-five miles away.

> Your
> loving son
> John Rock

All this fuss against the Government over Norway is nonsense. A lot of amateur strategists in the House are trying to blame Chamberlain for taking the advice of his service advisers. The Norwegians lost us that campaign and it was lost before it was ever begun.

The Battle for France commenced on 10 May 1940, with German troops taking the Allies by surprise by advancing through the Ardennes cutting off French and British troops that had advanced into Belguim. The German armoured divisions pushed the remaining Allied troops back as they withdrew to the coast.

John Rock
France

Sunday 12 May 1940
9.25 am

The White House
Cranleigh

Dear Mother

It was curious that I should have written to you on the 9th to say that I would be home on leave on the 20th. I'm afraid it is postponed again now. It was very bad luck on Brigadier Dempsey, who had one clear day at home, heard the news at breakfast on the 10th and was back here by seven o'clock the same evening.

The weather is still very fine and warm, though it is chilly in the evenings, and the country looks its best. I wish I could see your garden now, all the fruit trees must be looking grand. I should think you are kept busy with weeds sprouting everywhere.

I am glad Margaret is promoted to command a room and I hope her rate of pay has gone up accordingly. What else are we paying income tax for? I wonder how she will like working all night and sleeping all day. It is an awful shame to have to work indoors in all this weather but especially at night. Poor Mrs Thasby!

Our mess cook and staff are very good. They may not be able to cook like the French, but they do provide hot food when you want it. Last night I didn't get back to billets till eleven o'clock, having been out all evening and found the mess open and hot soup, fish and meat waiting for me. I was very grateful.

I'm afraid I can't give you any news. We are all thankful the scrap has come at last. One gets tired of waiting for it.

My love to Margaret
From your loving son John

CHAPTER FIVE

Bletchley Park And Ringway 1939 - 1940

THE COTTAGE, BLETCHLEY PARK

While John fought for his life in France, Margaret travelled from her Surrey home to Bletchley Park, a strange looking mansion nestled in the Buckinghamshire countryside. Once the home of Sir Herbert Leon, the house and its land was sold off at auction following the death of Lady Fanny Leon in 1937. After the sale of the property local builder Hubert Faulkner, planned a program of demolition and development but in April 1938 the estate changed hands once again. This time as part of a shadowy deal by Admiral Sir Hugh Sinclair, the Head of the Government Code and Cypher School (GC&CS) and Secret Intelligence Service (more commonly known as MI6).

It is not known what drew Admiral Sinclair to Bletchley Park but it may that as he sat smoking in his London club on 13 May 1937 reading The Times, he noticed the half page notice advertising the sale at auction of Bletchley Park and saw an ideal property for a war station - a base for GC&CS and SIS outside London in the event of war.

Station X, as it became known, was purchased out of Admiral Sinclair's own money to bypass departmental bickering between the War Office, Admiralty and Foreign Office over who should pay. He was a wealthy man and although the £6,000 price he paid was a substantial amount at that time, it was only a small part of the considerable fortune he left to his sister Evelyn Sinclair upon his death in December 1939.

Work started immediately to transform the estate into a suitable war station and a rehearsal under the cover name 'Captain Ridley's Shooting Party,' was carried out in September 1938, with parts of SIS remaining on site when GC&CS returned to Broadway Buildings, London in October.

When Margaret arrived at Bletchley Park on 15 April 1940, she entered the world full of eccentric university professors, mathematicians, chess champions and Foreign Office personnel that had been growing steadily since mid-August 1939, when the secret call up message 'Aunt Flo is not so well' was sent out to the first group of recruits waiting to make their way to Bletchley Park to break and decipher the coded messages of the enemy.

One of the eccentrics was the unique and brilliant Dilly Knox, a classics scholar of King's College, Cambridge, who had been recruited into Room 40, the Admiralty's codebreaking operation during World War 1. Here Dilly proved himself as an exceptional codebreaker and decided not to return to a quiet academic life at King's after the exhilaration and challenges of codebreaking. Instead he joined the newly formed Government Code & Cypher School in 1919 finding his way to the stable yard at Bletchley Park in August 1939.

Dilly settled his Enigma Research Section in a cottage located in the stable yard to work on breaking unsolved Enigma machine ciphers. It was here in Cottage No. 3 that Margaret met Dilly for the first in April 1940 and quickly showed her worth.

Training took several months, but not by Dilly, who was impatient and unorthodox when it came to training his staff. Mavis Lever (later Batey) arrived in May 1940 and recalls meeting Dilly for the first time, *'he was sitting by the window in wreaths of smoke and taking his pipe out of his mouth, he looked up and said "We're breaking machines. Have you got a pencil".'* After handing Mavis a series of papers he asked her to *'have a go'*. So Mavis joined Margaret and about seven others in the Research Section made up entirely of bright and academic women, known in the corridors of power as 'Dilly's Girls'.

While Margaret received letters from John about the invasion of Belgium, Bletchley Park received a flood of Enigma machine traffic intercepted from the invading German Army and Luftwaffe. Although broken, the intelligence derived from the messages was too late to help change the course of the battle in France.

At the end of August 1940 Dilly, already impressed with the work of Margaret and Mavis, put their names forward for a pay rise. For Margaret he wrote:

'Miss Rock is entirely in the wrong grade. She is actually 4th or 5th best of the whole Enigma staff and quite as useful as some of the 'professors'. I recommend that she should be put on to the highest possible salary for anyone of her seniority.'

Margaret received a promotion, earning the grade of 'Linguist', the closest a woman could get to being called a codebreaker. She also received an increase in salary, taking her to the top salary for a woman - £3.15.0 a week.

Dilly was always quick to attribute his successes to his team. He inspired his girls to be capable codebreakers and they came to look out for their *'wholly-minded'* mentor. They were readily on hand to help him when he stuffed his sandwiches into his pipe, rather than tobacco or mistaking the cupboard for the front door, and carry out regular hunts to find his glasses hidden under piles of papers or in his tobacco tin,. He is reported as saying, *'Give me a Rock and a Lever and I can move the Universe'*.

In October 1941 Margaret wrote to her childhood friend Norah Sheward, *'The poor grey matter is doing overtime. Sorry have no time for letters. Is this intense!*

This was a crucial time for the Cottage, as they tackled the complex Enigma cipher used by the Abwehr, the German military intelligence service. Only a few weeks after Margaret's postcard, Dilly made the vital step into understanding how the machine worked.

At this time Dilly was suffering from terminal cancer, and working through weeks of sleepless nights brought on a collapse in November 1941. A hopeful Dilly wrote to Margaret to say he would be off for a week but his cancer kept him away from Bletchley Park until he died in February 1943. He continued to work on the Abwehr problem at home, Courns Wood, Hughenden, Buckinghamshire, with Margaret acting as his assistant and liaison with Bletchley Park. Finally, the first Abwehr message was read on 8 December 1941.

Alistair Denniston, the operational head of Bletchley Park wrote to Stuart Menzies, the successor of Admiral Sinclair as Head of GC&CS and SIS about the team's success.

'Knox has again justified his reputation as our most original investigator of Enigma problems. He has started on the reconstruction of the machine used by the German agents and possibly other German authorities. He read one message on 8th December. He attributes the success to two young members of his staff, Miss Rock and Miss Lever, and he gives them all the credit. He is of course the leader, but no doubt has selected and trained his staff to assist him in his somewhat unusual methods.'

Breaking the Abwehr Enigma cipher gave Britain a huge advantage in the build up to the D-Day landings in June 1944. Reading the deciphered messages showed Churchill that Hitler had been fooled by the misinformation fed to him through double agents about the location of the Allies' invasion of Europe.

Mavis recalls that Margaret was also seriously ill from the end of 1941, suffering from pleurisy. Margaret gave up her billet at Friedenheim, Church Green Road (an address previously inhabited by Alistair Denniston and his family). She returned home to Cranleigh, and Mavis remembers visiting Margaret, possibly in January 1942, at a convalescence home near to her mother. She returned to work in June 1942, but her brother John felt she would need longer to recover. Mavis recalls that Alice *'bought or rented a house near the Park where she stayed. Sometime in the summer Margaret wanted me to meet John who was on leave and I had dinner with them.'*

With Margaret and Dilly away, Mavis and the rest of the section were under enormous pressure. Another talented codebreaker, Peter Twinn was asked to step into Dilly's shoes until his return and Keith Batey, moved from Hut 6 to find himself working with Mavis, who he would later marry.

By September Margaret was still struggling with the return to full health. Dilly moved away from the Abwehr codes and began working on an *'isolated problem'* with Margaret. It is strongly believed they were working on Russian ciphers, although Margaret never mentioned when she and Mavis were later working on Russian ciphers at Eastcote, the post war home of GC&CS, then named Government Communications Headquarters.

Shortly after Mavis Lever and Keith Batey married in London in November 1942, Dilly was taken into hospital. Margaret returned to Bletchley Park and Dilly wrote one final letter of thanks to his girls in January 1943.

On 27 February 1943 Dilly passed away at his home and was buried in the surrounding woodlands. For Dilly the war was over but for Margaret, Mavis and the thousands of staff at Bletchley Park, there were two years' of war left to decipher messages, retrieve and disseminate intelligence in an effort to help the fighting forces beat Hitler.

OFFICERS' MESS, RINGWAY

'We ought to have a corps of at least 5,000 parachute troops...I hear something is being done already to form such a corps, but only on a very small scale. Advantage must be taken of the summer to train these forces, who can, none the less, play their part meanwhile as shock troops in home defences. Pray let me have a note from the War Office on the subject'.

Winston Churchill to General Ismay,

War Office 22 June 1940

Major John Rock, who had recently returned from France, found himself summoned to the War Office on 24 June 1940 to hear he was to take charge of the military aspects of organising and development of an airborne force. John had an adventurous spirit with a strong background for organising troops and had the vision to interpret Churchill's wish to create a force that could be dropped into battle and easily get behind enemy lines. Despite his accomplished set of skills, John had no known personal experience other than a military glider demonstration in Budapest in August 1939.

When he arrived at Ringway, the requisitioned civil airfield located ten miles south of Manchester, he was met by flying ace, Pilot Officer Louis Strange, the man in charge of organising the Royal Air Force side. Finding it *'impossible to get any information as to policy or task.'* John started forging a force from nothing more than a parachute, a German helmet and four Whitley aircrafts. After a series of tests involving dummies, the first live test was carried out on 13 July 1940.

Meanwhile, Admiral of the Fleet Sir Roger Keyes and General Ismay worked on persuading Churchill that although the 5000 men were the ultimate aim, a force comprising 3,200 with 500 parachutists was a more achievable goal in the short term. The Air Ministry also talked of a glider regiment to exploit the ability of gliders to 'appear out of nowhere' and mount speed attacks, to which Churchill showed reticence unless the glider development '*represented a better capability than parachutists*'. Churchill wrote '*Press On*' on General Ismay's note setting out the numbers and decisions surrounding the airborne forces. The effect of the note reduced Churchill's dream of 5,000 parachute troops to 500 and prioritise gliders over parachutes.

New recruits into the Central Training School at Ringway were selected by a criteria that specified an ideal soldier with mental and physical fortitude. The mental strength of the early recruits were surely tested as they knew their instructors had as much experience as themselves. The instructors, including John, tried the techniques before the recruits. Captain Martin Lindsay recounts his experience of standing on a small platform preparing to be pulled backwards out of the aircraft as soon as he released the parachute.

'*I was undeniably frightened, though at the same time filled with fearful joy*'. Exhilaration replaced fear as he drifted down to the ground. '*I looked up and saw the silken canopy billowing in the air currents – a thing of beauty as the sun shone on and through it...I looked down, reflecting that this was certainly the second greatest thrill in a man's life.*'

The Central Training School experienced successful jumps but also jumps that went wrong. On 25 July 1940 July the first fatality occurred when the parachute of Driver Evans (RASC), failed to open correctly. There were forty six deaths during parachute training between July 1940 and March 1945, five of which occurred within the first year. Captain Lindsay recorded that '*morale in the commando was not good with distrust of the parachutes*'. After each accident the instructors always jumped before the recruits to boost morale.

John was also injured in 1941 (approximately August, although the date has not been substantiated) during a demonstration jump on a particularly windy day. His unconscious body was dragged across the ground, but did not result in broken bones. His letter about the accident suggests that he would stay in hospital for a few days. It was actually six weeks.

From September the training school became the Central Landing Establishment (CLE). The activities carried out were to remain a closely guarded secret. The troops were encouraged to speak as little as possible of their training. The CLE continued to work and found to get a parachute regiment ready it necessary to '*cover in six months the ground that the Germans have covered in six years*'. A difficult task with inadequate equipment and aircraft.

The Air Ministry's lack of enthusiasm for the project was not lost on the CLE staff and brought their frustrations to Churchill's attention during his visit on 26 April 1941. Churchill fumed at his Chiefs of Staff about the loss of a year that could have been used to develop a successful parachute training facility and invited them 'to make proposals for trying, so far as it is possible, to repair this misfortune.'

Finally progress was made. The No.2 Commando (renamed 11 Special Air Service (SAS) Battalion in October 1940) evolved and expanded into the 1st Parachute Brigade in September under Lieutenant General (later General) Richard Gale, followed a month later by the 1 Air Landing Brigade. Lieutenant General Frederick Browning was put in charge of the Airborne Division HQ at the end of October 1941 and held overall command for all Airborne forces. The CLE also received a name change to Airborne Forces Establishment (AFE). Within a newly-formed Army Air Corps there was to be a Glider Pilot Regiment, commanded by John Rock. Despite the name changes and restructure there was insufficient aircraft to adequately support the expanding force in training and operations.

The first Glider Training School was set up at Thame in December 1940 and the first recruits started training on 12 March 1941 with one Hotspur glider available for use. Three other training schools were established at various stages after December 1941 to further train recruits in the operational Horsa glider.

John was appointed Commanding Officer of the 1st Glider Regiment on 21 December 1941. With forty Army personnel from No.2 Commando he went to train in the art of flying gliders. While away, Major [later Brigadier] George Chatterton, was tasked with raising a regiment of 'total' soldiers, who could *'fly with the utmost skill and resolution.'* Each soldier *'must also be equally at home manning a Bren gun after landing, or driving a jeep, or firing a rifle, an anti-tank gun, or a mortar attained in the air.'* The desired skills were *'fearlessness, intelligence, robustness, flying experience with powered aircraft and flying experience with glider aircraft'.* The paratrooper was to be between nineteen and forty years old and weighing no more than 182 pounds. Their training involved intense physical fitness training, with tests to push their physical and mental abilities to the limits. Each paratrooper had to be prepared to land away from its unit and evade capture in enemy territory. Two thirds of the men who volunteered and passed the vigorous selection process for glider training reached the requisite military standard.

Lawrence Wright, an Air Force Officer in the Airborne Divison recalls the first night billeted with John describing him as *'small of stature, sparing of speech, and given to thinking before he answered,'* and found him *'a little forbidding'* when they were first billeted together. By the end of the first dinner the tension evaporated and Laurence *'learned a lot from Rock in the ensuing months.'*

By June 1942, John was based at No.4 GTS in Kidlington and received his wings on 9th June of that year. He wrote in September 1942 that there is a new 2nd Glider Regiment, commanded by his former second in command, George Chatterton. This letter is John's last letter and talks about the events to which he would give his life. He wrote on 20th September 1942 that he is *'concentrating on the problem of night-flying Hotspurs or rather night-landing Hotspurs. I think I have solved it and have had a most interesting job doing it.'*

A week later he took his solution to the night sky. Lawrence Wright also offers a first hand account.

'Each of its squadrons took turn to fly Hotspurs at Shrewton, and Robson's squadron was trying out a new reduced flarepath: one gooseneck flare that could be seen from some distance, and an L of resin lights to windward of it. They made an old mistake, in trying out two new things at the same time, for this was also their first night-flying with full ballast. Rock, watching the trial, said at the last moment come with you, Robby—and took the second pilot's seat. Whilst they made the circuit on tow, a swathe of fog drifted across the field, and the tug pilot had trouble in finding the flarepath. When he did see it, from only about 200 feet, he turned rather sharply towards it; the glider lost position, the rope slackened, then tightened and broke. Left so low and vertically over the landing strip, Robson rightly made no attempt to get on to it with a full load, but turned away to land on the open plain, where he should pick up the ground at the last moment with his nose-mounted navigation lamp. But he struck the top of one of the only line of telephone poles crossing the area, and the glider crashed upside-down. Robson was thrown out through the nose, but lived to fly again. Rock was trapped when the sandbag ballast shifted forward, and suffered fatal injuries.'

John died in hospital from his injuries on 8 October 1942. Margaret and Alice were devastated by the tragic loss. His memory has been immortalised in the history books as a pioneer in the early days of the parachute and glider forces. In 1945 the government's publication By Air to Battle – The Official Account of the British Airborne Division, paid tribute to John.

'The Glider Pilot Regiment had sustained a grevious loss by the death in October 1942 of [Lieutenant] Colonel Rock, killed in a glider which crashed during a night-landing experiment. The first to help in the creation of the new force, he had been throughout unsparing of himself, and he must be included in that select company of Englishmen, little known to their fellow-countrymen as a whole, who have rendered inestimatable service and taken no heed of the cost.'

Despite the political difficulties the airborne forces continued and went on to play its part in the World War 2. Men trained and lost their lives in operations such as Operation Torch (North Africa, November 1942), Husky (Sicily, July 1943, and Neptune (part of the D-Day landings in June 1944).

Margaret Rock
Bletchley

Sunday evening
September 1940

My dearest Mother,

I'm afraid it will be some time before you get this letter. I hadn't time to write this morning as I didn't get up till rather late, and now this won't get posted till tomorrow morning. I'm glad I was able to get you on the phone yesterday. I tried at 9.30, and Miss B tried during the morning, and they told her it would mean a wait of 3 hours. I hoped you would try yourself and find out that it was the telephone system that was wrong.

Well, as to my adventures on Friday night. I got to Euston by 8.15 - the raids had just started and there were guns beginning, which soon got much louder. There was no train before my 9.50, so I asked a porter where I should wait. He directed me to an archway, a very long one going between the tube station and one of the platforms. The passengers and railway staff (in tin hats) spent all their time there, and it felt very safe, and never shook, however near the bombs. I sat there for some time, and talked to an Irish girl, just landed in England. She is coming to stay with and help her sister, who is expecting a baby, and lives in Wallington in Surrey. She was completely bewildered; she had met her sister a time some days before and hoped someone would be there to meet her. But I expect the time hadn't been received yet. I told her to wait in the station or a shelter all night, and go on by herself in the morning. She has been here several times before, and said, without my asking her, what a difference she had noticed in English people - how sociable they are now. She thought it a great improvement. All the time a tremendous noise was going on, but no one took much notice of it, nor did we. A friendly porter came and told us to come with him if we'd like to see a fire, and from the entrance of the archway there was the whole sky lit up flaming red. It was quite near either St Pancras or Kings Cross Station. Meanwhile, though we didn't know it, a very heavy bomb had dropped on the railway, just past the first signal boxes and all the trains had been delayed for hours while the railwaymen repaired the damage, which they did, although the inferno was going on all the time.

At 9.45 I went and sat in my train (everything was pitch dark, only lit by the continual flashes and a few dim lamps). A Scotch porter came and sat in the carriage with me and talked till we were told by the loud speaker that there was a delay, we could go back to the shelter. His company was very comforting, it felt lonely and unprotected on the train. He had been one of the volunteers the previous evening and had walked up and down each line to look for unexploded bombs. I went back to the Irish girl and a porter got us some tea from the free railway canteen. At 11 o'clock a cry went round - all passengers leave the station. We didn't know where to go, but had the way to the nearest shelter described to us, and at last found it, in Euston Square. It was a now deathly quiet moment, luckily, only gunfire nearby, not bombs.

At 11.30 a railway man came and said the trains were running again, we could go back to the station. I took another farewell of the Irish girl and told her to stay where she was and try to sleep till the morning. I didn't like leaving her there alone, but I expect someone looked after her. Then again the handful of passengers got back to the station in the dark, I wishing I had a tin hat (and so did everyone else I expect). I was almost the only one for my train, and when I came to it I saw an Air Force man leaning out of a window so I joined him. I thought any company would be preferable to being alone on a night like that. The train didn't leave till after 2 o'clock so I was waiting in it 2 1/2 hours, all very alarming, as the glass roof didn't feel like any protection at all!

The Air Force man and I talked all the time, I had a synopsis of his life, which I could repeat if there were time and space now. He told me, to reassure me, that he was married! (It was pitch dark, as we had to have the blinds down, so I didn't know what he looked like, except for the lighting of a cigarette.) The bombs sometimes fell very near, the man said 100 yards or so away, he thought they were still trying to get the station. Sometimes the German planes would come lower and lower overhead, one would hear its drone over everything. The train shook sometimes, really by the time we left I felt quite glad to be alive. Though of course the railwaymen go through that every night. At last, at about 2.15, we left, and could go slowly over the damaged line. We had a very slow journey, stopping outside and at every station. He got out at Leighton Buzzard. He suggested meeting one evening, and took my name and address. I rather hope he loses it, but I felt it would have been churlish to refuse, after all we'd been through together. I got to Bletchley soon after 5.30, and went to bed till 8 o'clock. I must close now, as its 9.30 and I want to go to bed early again.

Miss B is supposed to be having a holiday, but is engaged at the moment coping with a fresh lot of children from London. Poor things, I'm glad they are coming away from London.

P.S I feel in a way rather relieved at having got over any first real bombing! My love to everyone. When I venture home again, which I'm afraid won't be for some time, I'll take leave from midday to midday, and avoid traveling at night.

Working back from next John's letter to Margaret mentioning her adventures at the weekend, it is estimated that this letter was written on Sunday 22 September 1940.

Bletchley Park Mansion

Cottage No.3 - Dilly's Research Section

John Rock
Officers Mess
RAF Station
Ringway
Nr Manchester

1 October 1940

Dear Margaret,

I heard from Mother today that you have been home for a weekend and had all sorts of adventures getting back to Bletchley again. What a time we live in, never a dull moment.

Life is still very quiet up here. We have not been bombed yet and only occasionally hear guns in the distance.

The weather is rather depressing. It has been very damp and misty for the last week, with a fog almost every night and a good deal of fine rain.

I am going out to dinner tonight with some people named Leaf and we shall play bridge afterwards. Lindsay has got in with a bridge playing set and goes out about five nights a week, but I value my sleep more and only go out one night a week. Actually this week is an exception as I am dining with Strange and others of our officers tomorrow night as well.

It is some time since I have been out to anything but a drinks party. You would be surprised at the amount of entertaining that goes on around here.

Anthony Eden had a look around this morning, and I had a few words with him. He flew over in a most luxuriously fitted out Flamingo. It had eight most comfortable easy chairs and its own lavatory.

I have just worked out a new War Establishment for us, by the way, we are now an Establishment and not a School and it comes to ten officers and seventy-nine men.

We are growing little by little, at present we are four officers and about forty men. Since I saw you I have got a parachute instructor, one Elliot, a young Territorial, quite a good chap, but unused to Army ways and a tactics instructor, one Bradish, a regular infantry officer, also quite young. Both are acting Captains. Elliott is billeted close to us in Mobberley and Bradish lives with his wife in Knutsford.

I have also got a new car, a beautiful 27 HP Humber Utility van, brand new. So now I have three cars.

Bower, whom I used to deal with at the War Office, has been relieved by Cassels and the latter has just returned after spending two nights with us. We always put up visiting officers in our billet.

Will you pass this letter on to Mother quickly, as I have a feeling that one is overdue.

Yours John Rock

Margaret Rock
Bletchley

Sunday 13 October 1940

Dearest Mother,

Just a line to send you all my good wishes for the 15th
and very many happy returns for your birthday. I hope to
post a small present this week. I wish I were going to be
at home to spend the day at home but I must think of you
here and drink your health in tea or some kindred liquor!

I have been spending a most lazy and pleasant Sunday
at home today, as I am starting night work for this week.
Last night I went to the canteen 7-11, and enjoyed it very
much though it was a most hectic rush, and most tiring -
but a complete change after our work here. There were 4
of us, Jean Haine and 2 Bletchley matrons, who knew all
about it. They were rather shocked at having newcomers
for Saturday night, but after the first few minutes of not
knowing where anything was we managed all night and
have been asked to go again.

Claire had told us that you could have anything you
liked to eat there, but luckily we had both found time 'to
get' something quick beforehand as there wasn't a second
when we could have eaten in!

There was no bacon or egg so everyone had sausages
and chips, and it was almost one person's job to keep the
potatoes peeled as there had been no time to do any ready
on the previous shift. Then there were the sausages and
baked beans on toast, and the toast burnt if you didn't
look! Many of the men are in a rush for their train which
are steaming in out of the station very noisily all the time.
The other helpers were very pleasant or rather, one I like
very much, the other was rather irritable, I daresay she
was tired. They all took turns at everything and of course

there was never ending washing up, which everyone did in spasms when there was a second to spare. Altogether a hectic rush, which was a nice change after much over-exercise of one's brains!

I am starting night-work as we have the girls who are there at night to do work for us and there is no one to see that the night things get done. I went in last night after the canteen and stayed till the 12 o'clock shift got settled and told them what to do. Then I came back and had Horlicks and bread and cheese; and didn't wake up this morning till 9.30. Miss B is away so I have had a thoroughly lazy day to myself. I took a jug up to bed, and then had a leisurely bath, and got down by 11 o'clock. There were things to clear up, and some washing and ironing, and then I sat in a deck chair outside the dining room door and had lunch and read the paper and nearly went to sleep. If this weather holds it will be lovely having these fine mornings to do what I like in.

I enjoyed my day in Northampton very much, and found it a much better place than I thought. The shops are very cheap, and I got pyjamas for 5/6, the most I could pay! We had a very good lunch and a glass of sherry each - altogether almost 2/- each - fish and chips and biscuits and cheese & lots of butter and coffee and for tea had buttered toast swimming in butter. We didn't go to the films but walked about the town and looked at the churches at great length - one a most beautiful Norman one, the loveliest in this district, I should think.

Please give everyone my love, including Aunt Ethel, who I hope is enjoying her visit to Cranleigh! I hope you have had your nights more peaceful lately.

With all my love to you

From Margaret

Alice Rock
White House
Cranleigh
Surrey

28 November 1940

My Dearest Margaret,

I am sitting over the fire and yet my hands are so cold I can hardly hold the pen - 11.30am. It feels quite a time since I wrote to you but our letters crossed. Its lovely to think you are coming next Wednesday. Don't forget to bring a little butter and marg, I'm very short. I'm very sorry you can't make it a weekend and have Norah. So glad you can sleep better in the day time if you don't return till Saturday it will seem a lovely long time.

The family returns Tuesday the 10th - they are not going to see Phil at all I gather. May liked Mr. M. very much, he wasn't any trouble. The batman cleaning shoes etc. I have 2 men in other the bedroom now, they are very different to Price, he was really polished. One of the new ones is a big country yokel, very shy and anxious not to annoy in any way. I hope it will last. The poor things they have been sleeping in the loft of a stable and had to run down steps for washing and shaving water, which was from the cold taps and the whole place was very damp. One has a very bad cold.

May hasn't heard any more of her brother but still are told not to give up hope. The fire is popping and Tony is worrying, wants to get into my chair and I won't have him.

The girl who served me in Gammons today had most of her fingers dead white with the cold. She had to ask me to help pull something out of a packet. I was sorry for her. I hope you will get the dressing gown you must want it in this weather. I enclose John's letter to me.

Fancy Berners St being roped off - it must be very bad for the Hotel. Nobody can get into Oxford St and his club damagaed. I saw a club had been hit and 2 people standing outside had been killed, and a man and his wife in the basement injured. The Budgett's aunt from Peaslake came to see them and said that a cord mine was in the field very near them. As it did not explode it was opened and found to be nothing more than concrete filling. We think made in Czeko. I hope a few more will come like that.

I had a letter from Connie [...] to thank me for the grapes. There was a good deal about her having no time to write, too much to do, needlework and she has Lakin on the correspondence!! A letter to Brian and Joan once a week.

Florence wrote that she had had to see a doctor, a bad cold and throat and general rundown. James had several visits to the dentist and no word on Charles. She was told that no letters posted July and August had arrived, no money sent for her and no letter received by the Bank Manager there, but may make that alright for her. She is anxious for news of us after all the wireless reports they get. Herbert has had the same flu as us, but is better.

I enjoyed Adele's visit very much. I am going to the pictures with Mrs Archibold on Saturday, "King Solomon's Mines". The Doctor won't go in the afternoon and she doesn't like the dark.

I haven't felt so well this week, dampness and cold gives me a nasty sort of indigestion and I haven't met Mrs French for weeks. She isn't ill for Nancy met her the other day. I suppose we shop at different times.

Much Love
    Your loving mother
      Alice M. Rock

(James & Charles Foster - Margaret's second cousins)

John Rock
Officers Mess
RAF Station
Ringway
Nr Manchester

Saturday 14 December 1940

The White House
Cranleigh

Dear Mother,

I apologise for chiding you for the infrequency of your letters. I am certainly in no position to cast stones.

We have had several days of severe frost and mist, when it has been freezing all day, but now it is raining again.

I have been quite busy again. Yesterday the C.I.G.S, Sir John Dill, visited us. We dropped two sticks of troops and landed five gliders for him and he was duly impressed. We gave him and General Finlaison lunch in mess, when he told us some interesting things about the fighting in Italy. One was that we have had enough troops in Egypt to do this for some time, but refused to move till the RAF had a move to four superiority over the Italians in aircraft.

We led him up to the office for 3/4 hour after lunch and put across our ideas for our force.

I have dined out the last two nights and refused to go out with Martin [Lindsay] this evening. We have a guest here, Cassels from the War Office, who is staying up the road with the Eckersleys, and dines with us and the Barclays and others have invited him out.

Robin Eubank came here a couple of days and spent a night. Unfortunately, I was very busy and could spend very little time with him.

We took him up in a Whitley, however, and he saw a

couple of sticks jump. I was one of them, my fourth jump. I had a perfect landing, as gentle as anything.

I went into Manchester for lunch today and had my hair cut and bought some urgent necessities but did not have time to get the dressing gown. I must go in again to do some other shopping and will buy it then.

I will certainly come home in Feb on leave, if Margaret can get here at the same time. I shall quite possibly be home for the night on Jan 5 or 6, perhaps both, as I am likely to be down that way on duty.

Our new house is quite comfortable now, and we have nearly finished moving in. We are going to give a house-warming party next Saturday, with about seventy guests.

The news in the papers is pretty good these days. Wavell has done awfully well and his gamble came off.

Hoping you and the Rock family are bearing up.

Your Loving Son

John

Alice Rock
White House
Cranleigh

Thursday 29 May 1941

My Dearest Margaret,

I do hope you didn't have too much trouble with all your parcels. Tony did enjoy his raw meat, it was easier than usual to cut into.

This morning was very cold until after dinner and I had a fire. Now it is warm and sunny out of the window and I am writing in the garden. Most of your orders have been carried out. Geraniums rooted up and dahlias cleared and taken into the shed. I have bought wall flower seeds and he is putting them in. Stocks and tomatoes I must buy as plants. Tomkin is asking 9/d each tomato plant. Luff advises my going to another shop before the other green grocers, kept by 2 women. The rain has brought things on splendidly. He thinks the berries are not frostbitten and lots of the currants are alright. He has planted the sugar beet! He proposes planting 3 tomatoes where they were before and the rest in front of the vinery.

I have had no letters since you left and I have sent the car insurance money. The Roosevelt speech made it as clear as diplomacy allows. I should say America is at war at this moment.

The garden is looking very lush, I did a little bit to it at 9.30 pm last night. Now Tony is lying prone beside me, very happy. I couldn't get him to bed last night, he kept running back and lying by the front door and May says he howled when we left him yesterday. I am so sleepy I must go in and sleep a bit and see if the post bag brings anything.

No letters so nothing to add. Lovely evening.
Best Love

Your loving Mother

Alice. M. Rock

Luff very depressed as to our fruit. Frost has done its worst, hardly any blackcurrants left - an expert's opinion is that no apples this year, frost attacked the trees before they flowered.

Alice Rock
White House
Cranleigh
Surrey

12 July 1941

My dearest Margaret,

Thanks for your letter and John's, I wish we had had your heavy rain, never a drop for 3 weeks though it has looked like it often.

What a long ride to Northampton in such weather, shopping seems bad everywhere. Connie and I went to see "The Farmer's Wife" here, not as good as the play.

So, the probabilities about Wales is only for con[serving] water, but we use all dish water in case we empty the tank. Mr Luff says he used 40 gallons on Thursday, the fruit and veg are getting very hard, peas are dried up. May has bottled 5lbs of gooseberries and 2 of red currants and Connie made 3lb gooseberries into 5lb jam, all was very successful, much more so than need to.

Tony is better but still has a discharge from his eyes, we have prevented him going into the long grass and Nancy wrote very cheerfully I thought. I enclose the cutting about the Vance Jones. I rather hope he had to suffer some discomfort. I never thought Phyllis would be popular out there.

I hope your gramophone will be a success. Don't pay less than £6 something.

We are in the garden except at Terries where the dining room is cooler. How lovely you are coming on 20th, I don't mind how late, it will be cool and light. I feel a bit tired and am looking forward to Wednesday it is hard work when there is only myself to listen to the talk. Adele came to supper last night and leaves tomorrow afternoon, she is a great help just now it is awfully hot in the garden and I am writing in the dining room. Adele said she wanted to lie out and sleep but Connie's tongue has gone on in a dull monotony ever since. Adele bought me a lot of food (rations) very tender steak, 7 eggs, butter, marg and bacon, I wouldn't take her sugar or tea. We are rather over done with food this weather. I had provided a bit of salmon last night and a chicken for tomorrow and some mutton in the house.

Wasn't it strange - Mrs Crowhurst came to tea yesterday she and her husband were at Bordon on the Water in April and stayed at St Kevins and loved it, he had a brother at the Aerodrome there.

Alice Rock

John Rock
Officers Mess
R.A.F Station
Ringway
Nr Manchester

Wednesday 6 August 1941

Mrs Rock
Friedenheim
Church Green Road
Bletchley
Bucks

Dear Ma,

I'm afraid my last letter was rather late, so I write a bit sooner this time. I have just come back from a very pleasant night in Yorkshire.

I had not had a change for a long time and needed it badly. Norman and I went up north of Thirsk by car to visit an armoured division. We stayed the first night at divisional headquarters, and had a number of discussions about the use of parachutists and the next night with a tank regiment, the 24th Lancers and went up with them on the moors to watch tank training. It was windy and cold and wet, but a pleasant change from Manchester. I was allowed to drive a heavy tank, the thing I have always wanted to do.

I also went for a ride in one, sitting in the current. Luckily, I wasn't driving, for we ran into a deep ditch and ditched the tank, also breaking the arm of an officer who was in there with me. You got an awful jolt when the tank pulls up suddenly on its nose.

We were visited by two generals today, Rawson in the morning and Adam in the afternoon, so I didn't get much work done. Tomorrow evening I hope to get a game of squash with Bradish.

I hope to get your birthday present tomorrow. I may look in on you and Margaret Tues, Wed or Thurs, my plans are a bit vague yet, but I am going down south soon.

It is time for bed,

Your loving son John

John Rock
Wittington Hospital
West Didsbury
Near Manchester

Saturday August [1941]

Mrs Rock
The White House
Cranleigh
Surrey

Dear Mother,

Just a line to reassure you as to my condition. Martin told me that he wrote and told you I had been sent here.

The fact is, I did a descent on Thursday, with all my Instructors and six RAF Instructors, as a demonstration to the assembled troops as to how to do it, preparatory to their doing it themselves next day.

It was a windy day and worst of all, gusty, and so I came out all right and my chute opened, after I had descended a few hundred feet, and mighty gust of wind came, carried my shoot away and started me swinging and I was still swinging when I reached the ground. From the bruises, I must have landed on my left hip and then hit my head on the ground, because I was knocked out and dragged 150 yards before they could reach me. They sent me here suffering ostensibly from concussion, but it was a very slight and my head is quite all right now, though my hip is still very painful. It was not such a bad knock as I had at school, as I had a headache for the week after that.

I was x-rayed this morning, my hip, head and arm and nothing is broken. My arm was only scratched, also my face, owing by supposed to being dragged. Anyway, there is nothing much the matter with me, and I can walk with an effort, though I'm not supposed to.

In fact, if left to my own devices, I should go back to work tomorrow, as it is, in the clutches of a hospital, I expect to be here for all five days more.

I find a civilian hospital slightly slower, more red tape ridden than an army one, as for women with a little bit of authority, they have to be seen to be believed. I am in open rebellion, but really they are very nice and more efficient than male orderlies.

I am in a small room to myself, just off a large ward. This has many obvious advantages, there were of course it is still, one misses the hundred and one goings on in a large ward which help to relieve the tedium.

By the way mother, don't think of coming up here to see me, because I am quite well, and is liable to be out quite soon and practically certain to beginning a spell of leave when I come out.

I saw a copy of a letter from the War office to Western command HQ today, saying it was strongly recommended that I should be given ten days leave on being discharged from hospital. It went on "as it is likely that he will regard this as unnecessary it is requested that you will see that it is enforced."

You might tell Margaret that I shall be on leave soon, so that she can warn her people. I will let you have the date as soon as I can, I expect it will be in a weeks time.

I am writing today to my insurance company, asking them to ensure the car and send you the certificate and cover note. Then you might get it licensed for me. If you can get it licensed before the end of August so much the better, you could get the petrol coupon for August and have the petrol put in my tank. One can't keep one months coupons and leave them to the next month now.

There is a chap next door who never stops moaning and groaning. He must be a damn nuisance to everybody.

Lindsay has been up to see me in Wing Commander Blackford was up this evening, so I am not being neglected.

I have been lent a portable wireless set and am about to turn on the 6 o'clock news, so I will close. I have lots of literature and quite comfortable.

Your loving son John

John Rock 1942

Margaret Rock
Bletchley

Wednesday morning

Circa August 1941

The White House
Cranleigh

My dearest Mother

What a budget of letters from you and John, all arriving together. You must have had a terribly anxious time waiting to hear more. How happy you must have felt when the letter from John arrived. Poor John, what a nasty accident, how infuriating for it to happen in the middle of this demonstration.

I can easily take my weeks leave at the beginning of September. Its the middle that would be more difficult for me, but not many will be away the first week. So I will arrange to come home on the Saturday, Sunday or Monday night accordingly as I hear from John and you. I think Sunday or Monday are better, as Saturday is such a crowded day traveling, and if John has 10 days, he is sure to overlap with me anyhow. How lovely it will be to manage a leave together. I just feel I could enjoy another week now!

I'm sorry to hear you have had bombs in Cranleigh. I hope no one was hurt. By the law of averages, you shouldn't have any more, as it must have been chance. We had our nearest one last night, I don't think quite in Bletchley. I was in the bath so got out and dried myself quickly. One feels more able to cope with emergency dry and clad! But there were no more.

If Aunt should go to Sylvia's wedding, I might go from here. My chief reason against was that there wouldn't be much petrol left for my weeks leave late in the month - a purely selfish reason. Also, I feel rather tired these 2 days and didn't feel I could cope with new hats and arrangements. But I feel much better now. All Monday I felt more tired and depressed than I have done for ages, I couldn't think why, but on Tuesday I was perfectly alright again. I went to the pictures, which were rather feeble, as a mild relaxation, and all the way home heard a German plane flying about, and almost 15 searchlights trying to pick him up. They didn't succeed and he dropped some bombs away to the south of us soon after 11 o'clock. It was a most impressive sight.

I must write to John, and must close now. With my love to you all and I hope I shall be home soon for a week.

Your loving Margaret.

P.S I suppose the nurses insist on washing John and he doesn't like it!

John Rock
Royal Air Force
Mildenhall
Bury St.Edmunds

Tel: Mildenhall 2146

29 September 1941

Dear Mother,

Just a line to let you know all is well. I was very busy at Camberley after I left you, so busy that I was unable to get over again. The week went well and was very successful. I went back to Ringway by a Mansfield, where I spent a night with the 1st Parachute Brigade, spent one night at Ringway and came straight on here next morning to help with the Army manoeuvres. This is my second night here and I think I may be here another night and then move to Duxford, Louth or Cambridge, for another two nights.

We have not dropped any parachutists yet, but I hope we shall do so tomorrow. It is quite interesting and I am fairly busy.

I expect to go straight from here to Farnborough, when the manoeuvres are over and shall probably spend a night there, but I rather doubt if I shall have time to get over to see you. I will if I can. I shall being engaged in some very technical stuff and container design.

I had a letter from you just before I left. My day in London was quite successful, but I didn't do any shopping.

Poor Margaret, she had a lot of trouble with the car.

Give the rats my love,

Your loving son John

John Rock
Officers Mess
R.A.F Station
Ringway
Nr Manchester

Sunday 4 October 1941

Mrs Rock
The White House
Cranleigh

Dear Ma,

I got back from Middenhall, via Farnborough last night, after a very pleasant week. The weather could not have been kinder to our manoeuvres. It was warm and sunny all the time. We dropped about 250 paratroops altogether and it was quite a success. We had twelve aircraft, and on one occasion dropped a hundred men at once.

I got to Farnborough in the evening and left again to return here after lunch next day, so, as I feared, did not have time to go over and see you.

During the week I motored a thousand miles, in a very comfortable 25 HP Vauxhall, lent to me by command HQ.

Having been away now nearly three weeks on end I shall find plenty of work in the office, but I fear I shall have to go up to London tomorrow night for a conference. I am a little tired of travelling. It was very pleasant at Middenhall, in a nice bracing climate, as a change from Cheshire.

I had an interesting time at Farnborough; after doing my business, I looked round the hangars and saw all sorts of a/c [aircraft], including a M.E.109F, a S.V.88, a Liberator, a Whirlwind. I saw the Typhoon and the Hurricane II at Gloucester.

I cannot see my next week's leave in sight yet, but will take it as soon as I can manage it.

Your loving son John

Margaret Rock

7 October 1941

Sub: N. Sheward T
Sub J Macklin A.T.S
17 White Ladies Road
Bristol

The poor grey matter is doing overtime. Sorry have no time for letters. Is this intense!

Thanks a lot for everything.

M. T

Just received a parcel thanks a lot

The 'T' after Sheward on the address appears to be a sort of symbol, as is the 'T' following the M. The postcard is in Margaret's handwriting and has a photograph of the New Forest, Hants on the reverse side.

John Rock
Officers Mess
R.A.F Station
Ringway
Nr Manchester

Thursday [circa October 1941]

Friedenheim
Church Green Road
Bletchley
Bucks

Dear Margaret

I got back by about 7.15 after dull journey, except for a snow-storm near Lichfield and a puncture at Newcastle.

It snowed here the night I got back and has snowed intermittently ever since.

As usual, I fine a good deal of work waiting for me to do, but feel very much better for my rest. There is no sign of my attack of 'flu'.

Our friends, who were all going to the theatre in separate cars, all arrived there safely with most of their belongings, only one of the cars was rather late.

There was practically no audience, just a few country people, but the scenery and costumes were beautiful.

Unfortunately, the bus which had been arranged to take them home did not turn up, though they waited some time for it, so those who did not decide to stay in the village were faced with rather a long walk home.

The critique of the play was difficult to follow, though the illustrations were good. I have not really made up my mind about it yet, but I am afraid that it was, on the whole, a bad notice.

I shall be very interested to hear what your own friends

thought of it, if you have heard from them. The only good notice in the paper was about the efforts of another company under the same management who were doing a vaudeville show in another small town about fifteen miles away.

I shall probably be going up to London on Sunday night for a day or two and shall hope to get away from the snow there. Mrs Gough tells me that, last March, the snow was so deep here that, one morning the neighbours had to come and dig her out, before she could open the front door.

I do hope Mother's cough is better and that you yourself are alright now.

Don't forget to ask Mother for my equipment and revolver. I was a fool to forget that. If you drop it in at Boodles for me (on the left, going down St James St) , I will pick it up, or get someone at the W.O [War Office]to collect it and send it up here. Have it unloaded first.

Yours

John Rock

John Rock
Officers Mess
R.A.F Station
Ringway
Nr Manchester

Friday [circa October 1941]

Dear Ma

I am very pleased to hear that you are feeling better and that the doctor has pronounced you sound in limb if not in mind.

I have not very much news for you. Martin is back from leave and I have been dining out a good deal and consuming lots of drink. We are having a little dinner-party here tomorrow night. Nancy Leaf and Audrey are going to check our accounts, which are rather high.

It is mild and blustery weather with frosts at night. The crocuses are coming up in the garden and we have two bowls of narcissus in our sitting-room.

A major from the War Office cam up yesterday and spent the night on the floor in my room. We were going to stay down about sixty miles south of here, to watch a parachute exercise, but it had to be cancelled, owing to bad visibility.

We occasionally get a day warning now, but never a night one. Manchester had a few bombs about lunch-time today.

I had some news of our actor friends today. Most of them have been forced to stay down in the country, but five of them are still on a working-tour. One of them got hurt, but the rest, I think, are intact. All those on tour are old Chatham friends of mine.

I am sure now that I left my gun at Mildenhall and am waiting to hear from them. Please send my fire-arms certificate and that sketch map that Dora finally sent me, if you have not thrown it away.

No more

Your loving son

John

Margaret Rock is sat on the far right with Dilly Knox stood behind. circa 1940 - 1943

Dilly Knox
Courns Wood
Hughendon
Bucks

Monday 10 November 1941

Miss M Rock
Bletchley Park
Bletchley
Bucks

Dear Margaret,

I have been laid up more or less-nothing serious - for the last four days. I shall count this as sick leave and not return for week or so unless statistics beetles space double calculations etc, are all finished earlier and I don't see how they can be. Let me know sometime about Thursday if anything breaks.

Love to all

Dillwyn Knox

Alice Rock
Redcliffe Hotel
Paignton
South Devon

6 May 1942

Coy Commdander N Sheward
A.T.S
Drill Hall
Old Coulsdon
Surrey

We are having lovely weather and M[argaret] is out all day, beautiful garden here, and rock garden and little parks about, she never need get over tired. It is a very long job, getting back strength. She is longing to go back home to see the garden and I'm afraid she will say to look in it before she ought.

We went into Torquay one afternoon to a violin recital, which did her good.

I hope you are enjoying your new job. Our love

A.M.R

John Rock
Kidlington

Monday 8 June 1942

Mrs Rock
The White House
Cranleigh

Dear Mother

I receive my wings tomorrow, the general is coming up here to present them to No 1 course.

The weather has been and still is perfect, in fact almost too hot.

On Friday we all went into Oxford to bathe. The water was lovely. We bathed in the baths in a backwater of the Thames and lay out and sunbathed afterwards.

On Saturday, I flew up to Hendon and then took the tube up to town to attend another officer's wedding. I found time to have my hair cut and visit the War Office and then flew back in the time for dinner. Today I flew up to Northolt, on the west of London and back. During the week I have paid a visit to Derby and to Netheravon, so I have been getting about a good deal.

I am sorry Margaret will be gone when I come on home, but I can well understand how keen she must be to get back to work. I still think though that she would be well advised to stay longer, judging by the experience of one of my officers, who had much the same trouble a year ago and was only pronounced fit to fly a month ago.

I have heard from one or two friends at Ringway lately. They are all without servants and finding life much harder work than it used to be, but they say they are happier now.

I have no more news and am very sleepy after a long days flying.

Your loving son
John

John Rock
1st Glider Regiment
Army Air Corps
Home Forces

20 September 1942

Cliff Side Hotel
Newton Ferress
South Devon

Dear Margaret,

I am afraid I have not written to you for an awfully long time. I expect it is I who owe you a letter.

I had a very pleasant fortnight in Brize Norton, flying Horsas. They are not difficult to fly and in spite of the size, are remarkably manoeuverable. The mess was just like a peace time mess, such as I have not lived in since the war started. It boasted two squash courts. I found a packet of work waiting for me when I got back, but have got through most of it now and am concentrating on the problem of night-flying Hotspurs or rather night landing Hotspurs. I think I have solved it and have had a most interesting job doing it.

We have a second regiment now, commanded by my late second in command, George Chatterton. We still both share the same camp, an unsatisfactory arrangement for both of us.

My new camp at Larkhill is building and to look at it you would think it was finished, but most of the essential things, like drainage, cookhouses, baths and ablutions have barely been started. I don't expect to get into it before December or January.

In the meantime, I am expecting to remove the 1st Regiment from here, into tents. It will take a bit of getting used to.

Martin Lindsay is on his way home from abroad. He had a difference of opinion with his Brigadier. Martin was exonerated by a Court of Inquiry, but they were both sacked. Such is life.

I do hope you are enjoying yourself down in Devon. I send this home for redirection. I also hope that Dilly will soon be restored to health and you too.

      Yours
        John Rock

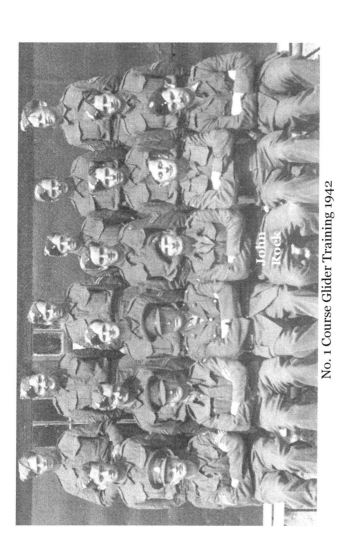

No. 1 Course Glider Training 1942

John Rock

In His Majesty's High Court of Justice
The Principal Probate Registry at Llandudno

BE IT KNOWN that **John Frank Rock** of Cliff Crescent North Queensferry in the County of Fife Scotland, formerly of 30 St Marys Mansions Paddington, London N.2 and base of Lloyds Bank Limited, 6 Pall Mall London S.W.1 Lieutenant Colonel in H.M. Army died on the **8th day of October 1942** at Tidworth in the County of Wilts domiciled in England

AND BE IT FURTHER KNOWN that the date hereunder written the last Will and Testament

(a copy of whereof is hereunto annexed) of the said deceased was proved and registered in the Principal Probate Registry of His Majesty's High Court of Justice and that Administration of the all Estate which by law devolves to and vests in the personal Representative of the said deceased was granted by the aforesaid Court to -

Margaret Alice Rock of White House, Cranleigh in the County of Surrey Spinster sister if deceased the sole Executrix named in the said Will.

And it is hereby certified that an Affidavit for the Inland Revenue has been delivered herein, it is shown that the gross value of the said Estate in Great Britain (exclusive of what the deceased may be possessed of as a Trustee and not beneficially) amounts to £3,273.18.2 and that the net value of the personal estate amounts to £3,273.18.2.

Dated the 9th day of January 1943
Registrar

Extracted by Gilbert H White & Co
3 Bank Buildings Cranleigh

Last Will and Testament

I John Frank Rock of Cliff Crescent, North Queensferry in the County Fife, do hereby revoke all will and testamentary instruments heretofore by me made and declare this to be my last will whereof I appoint my sister Margaret Alice Rock sole Executrix of this my will.

I hereby give and bequeath to my sister Margaret Alice Rock for her own use absolutely all my estate and effects both real and personal whatsoever and wheresoever and of what nature and quality so ever.

I also give and bequeath my sister Margaret Alice Rock for her own use absolutely all monies derived from life policies.

Signed by me this fourth day of November Nineteen Hundred and Thirty.

J.F.Rock

Signed by the testator in our joint presence and signed by us at his request and in his presence an in the presence of each other

Witnesses to the above Will

E. A. Stansfield
Widow
Cliff Crescent
North Queensferry

Christina Higgins
Spinster
Cliff Crescent
North Queensferry

Martin Lindsay
Raby Lodge
Haywards Heath

17 October 1942

Dear Mrs Rock

I enclose the appreciation of John which I sent to "the Times" on Tuesday and which I shall hope they will print though perhaps at a reduced length. There was just a short paragraph about him at the news ticker which I read at the club on Tuesday, only saying that he had been killed and that he was the first soldier to qualify both as a parachutist and as a glider pilot and that he was C.O of the glider pilots regt nothing more.

I miss him a lot. I didn't know if he told you that his regimental buttons were a present from me on leaving Ringway last year.

With deepest sympathy once more in your terrible loss.

yours

Martin Lindsay

The appreciation was very short, to increase its chances of being published.

Obituary sent to The Times

Major Martin Lindsay
Boodle's
St James's Street
S.W.1

Lieut. Col. J.F.Rock, R.E

The death from a gliding accident of John Rock is not only a great shock to his friends but a serious loss to our airborne forces, in the technical development of which he played a leading part from the start. In June 1940, Colonel Rock was chosen to start parachute troops and took his share of the risks and mishaps of the early experiments which have now made the landing of soldiers by parachute comparatively safe. Military gliders grew up around him and when a Glider Pilot Regiment was formed, he was appointed to command it. He still continued to do more than his share of new development work in spite of at least one serious accident, which might have deterred a less gallant man. He died in a military hospital in October from multiple injuries received in a crash a fortnight before when making another glider flight of an experimental nature.

From the Imperial Service College Rock went to Woolwich and was commissioned in the Royal Engineers in 1925. His early career as a sapper subaltern included a period as a Garrison Engineer, construction work in Ceylon, and being an instructor at the School of Engineering. In 1937 he went to Germany and obtained his first class interpretership a year later, shortly before going to the Staff College. During the fighting in France and Belguim he was Brigade Major of the 11th Infantry Brigade. Colonel Rock's father lost his life at sea as a naval surgeon in the last war; his mother, to whom he was devoted, was a great influence in his life. He was unmarried.

His death will be deeply felt because of three qualities which he possessed to quite an exceptional degree: strength of character, ability and personal charm. It is no exaggeration to say that those of us who served under him came to love him. His work goes on and the better for his inspiration, for he set us an example which we shall never forget.

M.L

Dilly Knox
Courns Wood
Hughenden
Bucks

3 January 1943

Dear Margaret
Mavis
Rachel etc
Denys
Peggy

Very many thanks for your, and the whole section's, very kind messages of congratulations. It is of course, a fact that the congratulations are due the other way and that awards of this sort depend entirely on the support from colleagues and associates to the Head of the Section. May I, before proceeding, refer them back.

It is, I fear, incumbent upon me at the same time to bid farewell. For more than ten years, I have taken up with A.G.D. the position that (a) there is no proper distinction between research cryptography and cipher and intelligence work, (b) that it is as improper to ask a person of any degree of education to run a key-setting bureau, as to ask him or her to run a typewriting section, (c) that it is impossible to edit or translate satisfactorily without a precise knowledge of the cipher in question, (d) latterly we have recruited during and shortly before the war from the Universities; and Academic tradition does not understand the idea that a half-fledged result should be removed from the scholar who obtains it and handed over to another. The discoverer loses all interest in further discovery and the recipient has no interest in the offspring of another's brain. Still more doubtful is the case of 'Research'. Until we know who will handle and circulate any result we get, the irrertum aurum of our search will very probably be sic melius situm.

I have recently arranged with the authorities to attempt a line which should give a wider scope though it will be of far less importance. In bidding farewell and in closing down the continuity but not, I hope, the traditions of the Cottage, I thank once more the section for the unswerving loyalty, Theirs I remain

Affectionately

A.D. Knox

This letter is from The National Archives at reference HW25/12

CHAPTER SIX

Cold War Code Breaking at GCHQ

When war ended in Europe many people at Bletchley Park returned to their homes and families. Others continued to work with the Americans until Japan surrendered in August 1945 before returning to their pre-war lives. Official records recording the number of staff show that only seven members of ISK remained in August 1945.

The Government Code & Cypher School was looking towards the next threat - Russia. It was also assessing the remaining staff to move from Bletchley into the next phase of the organisation as the Government Communications Headquarters (GCHQ) in Eastcote. The new GCHQ would still come under the control of Stuart Menzies as Head of GCHQ and SIS, but it would be a completely separate organisation and employ 260 men and women, with at least 200 'first class minds'.

The new organisation moved to the former Bletchley Park outstation located on the outskirts of London and close to the General Post Office (GPO) Research Department where Colossus, the first programmable computer had been built to decipher the messages of Hitler's High Command.

To prepare for the move a series of memos were circulated setting out information about the ideal candidates, their pay and a schedule of moving. Margaret was an ideal candidate. Her work at Bletchley Park was rewarded with becoming a Member of the Order of the British Empire (MBE) honours award in 1945. She also had experience working on Soviet ciphers and so was already had an advantage in understanding the forthcoming conflict.

Mavis Batey believes Margaret had been working on Soviet ciphers with Dilly during his last years at Courns Wood. Although Margaret was secretive about the work and Mavis never asked, it had appeared to Mavis that Margaret started with a greater understanding of the problem when they worked at Eastcote together.

The move to Eastcote was scheduled for early 1946 to be carried out in four waves. Peter Twinn's department was one of the first to go. The tight schedule left little time between the transfer to Eastcote and starting in their new roles. There was no time to rest, the Cold War had begun.

Margaret never married, and neither did her childhood friend, Norah Sheward. They remained close through World War 2 as their lives and careers took separate turns. As the 1940s drew to a close, Margaret and Norah drew closer to their fifties. As they were both single with aging mothers, they decided to live together, with Norah taking on the role of carer and Margaret continuing to work.

During the 1940s Alice moved to Wimbledon but signs of dementia became apparent. By the time Alice died on 10 April 1951, she was staying with Margaret and Norah at their home in Ickenham, Middlesex. Shortly after Alice's death, GCHQ moved to its new location in Cheltenham, Gloucestershire. Margaret moved with the organisation settling just over the county boundary in the picturesque village of Bredon, Worcestershire in 1954.

Margaret and Norah socialised with other GCHQ colleagues, such as Jean Perrin (formerly Hazelrigg), another of Dilly's Girls form The Cottage. Jean moved to Cheltenham with her husband Kenneth who had continued to work at GCHQ. Margaret and Norah were also very musical, playing violin and piano in a quartet made up of their work colleagues.

Margaret retired from GCHQ on 7 July 1963. She once again signed a section of the Official Secret Act specifically written for those leaving the organisation. It prevented her from talking about her post war work but after years of keeping the details of her work private, Margaret found the secrecy easy.

10 Downing Street
Whitehall

28 May 1945

Personal & Confidential

Miss M.A.Rock

Madam,

I am desired by the Prime Minister to inform you that it is his intention, on the occasion of the forthcoming list of Birthday Honours, to submit your name to the King with a recommendation that he may be graciously pleased to approve that you be appointed a Member of the Order of the British Empire (M.B.E).

Before doing so, the Prime Minister would be glad to be assured that this mark of His Majesty's favour would be agreeable to you, and I am to ask that you will be so good as to communicate with me accordingly at your earliest convenience.

Yours faithfully

I.M.Martin

Alice Rock
White House
Cranleigh
Surrey

31 May 1945

c/o Mrs James
The Chestnuts
Denbigh Road
Bletchley

I had just sat down to write you when the postman brought your letter. Oh my darling I am so glad and proud that you have been chosen for a decoration, you certainly deserve one. I can't help tears coming when I remember the two who would have rejoiced with you, I remember your Father repeatedly saying "she must go to University" and how John even as a small boy told everybody how clever you were. They must be rejoicing with us now, one can't tell.

How glad Mr Knox would have been and how proud of you Professor Hilton will be.

I rather hope the fools plans will allow you to come home earlier. I should love to talk about it, but only to you. I have kept a good many secrets. I shan't have to wait long.

M.B.E is the highest of the "Empire" range I think, and I believe King's birthday is a fixed date in June. I hadn't really any news and your news has put out of my mind everything else. I hope the "birthday" is early in June. What a day it will be when you can tell people or they may see it in the paper, but how few made it through the long lists!

All my love to you
From your loving and proud Mother.

Alice Rock
White House
Cranleigh

Sunday 3 June 1945

Miss Rock
C/O Mrs Garner
The Chestnuts
Denbigh Road
Bletchley
Bucks

My dearest Margaret,

It seems more like a month than a week since you left. Weather has been bad, I've only had tea once an that's all in the garden and often I have had a fire and the lamp.

Miss Bush and her sisters came to tea today, we kept the ball rolling with stories till past 6. Tony laid in the conservatory through tea time (the door being open) they chose their own day (on Saturday) so I couldn't order a cake but Mrs Crockett made a lovely sponge.

Your news was so exciting, I hate having to wait, I can't phone you about it. I haven't seen any announcement in the "Times". All the news in the paper is very serious I think actual peace and quiet is a long way off yet!

I have heard more grumbling since peace was signed than before.

May was having lunch with a friend at the Black Horse, Horsham and saw Mary Thorp (I think with a friend). Mutual recognition and a chat followed.

Mr Crockett has put something on the back gate to prevent thieves getting in at night. Mr Luff came this afternoon to see the tomatoes and couldn't open the door, he went round to the front. A good thing it works.

Monday morning - Honours are not in the papers today! But a letter has come from you from the car insurance people. On one paper it says "your motor vehicle licence will be sent as soon as possible, you may use the car without it and carry the slip of paper with you, petrol coupons enclosed". On the printed paper they have scratched through the line which says you have paid the licence.

I have the envelope still on my desk marked car licence but I am sorry to say I have forgotten if I ought to have done anything.

Well I think I will enclose all the papers they sent and keep the petrol coupons. Shall I get Butcher to clean the car before you come?

My love to you.
    Your loving mother

    Alice M.Rock

15 June 1945

My dear Margaret

May I offer my most warm and cordial congratulations on your decoration?

It is good to see this public recognition of the remarkably distinguished work you have done here; and equally good to know that there is not a single member of the Section who will not be frankly delighted at the news. There never was a clearer case. You have been pre-eminent among those few people to whom we owe, fundamentally, the whole success of our work in these hard unnatural years; we, your colleagues, have long known this - it is good to see it openly acknowledged.

My best wishes to you, and again my most sincere congratulations.

Yours Ever

Denys Page

Denys Page succeeded Oliver Strachey as the Head of ISOS (Illicit Services Strachey). It dealt with the hand ciphers used by Abwehr. He was promoted to Assistant Director Illicit Signals (AD IS) in March 1944 with direct responsibility for ISK and ISOS.

Margaret Rock GHQ Codebreaker 1950s

London

15 June 1945

Miss M.A. Rock, M.B.E

Dear Miss Rock,

I wish to send you my congratulations on the award of the M.B.E. which has today been granted to you.

You have been employed on work of a highly technical nature, the results of which have been of the greatest value.

I am very pleased to see that official recognition has been given to you and I am satisfied that this award has been richly deserved.

Yours sincerely

S.G Menzies

Stuart Menzies, Head of MI6

Alice Rock
White House
Cranleigh
Surrey

Friday 15 June 1945

c/o Mrs James
The Chestnuts
Denbigh Road
Bletchley

My dearest Margaret

It was a great disappointment not seeing the announcement in the papers today. Thanks for your letters, I'm so glad your troubles ceased at Cranleigh. I am glad Peter has done well in London. One can't make plans just now. Poor you with those awful bites. I must ask Nancy if she got them too. So glad you are coming next week. What about Mrs Garner it would be easier before the work people start inside. I hope that wont be till July.

Weather improving, we couldn't sit in the garden but now nearly 5pm sun is everywhere. Shooey brought everything for the glass and frost back mint and lots of roses and flowers, she has Miss Taylor coming for certain. Miss T is being turned out of her place now and Shooey has no place to take her. Rather worried like everybody.

As I write you will to having your party, I hope it will be a great success. Sure to be plenty to eat and drink. What a lovely idea of Mary Kelly's to paint the invitations. I will tell Nancy you would like to get more bites. Miss Bush left today. Waited to see "Arsenic and Old Lace" yesterday, they asked me to go too. I did and thought it waste of time and money. Most revolting thing I have seen. I think you warned me against it but I forgot.

I don't see any way to go to Adele's. I have written and said I might be able to go after next week. Next week I must have the chimney swept before the work people start inside. I can't be away with men coming in and out. Tony has to be looked after. He is constipated every other day. When he has taken medicine he is only right for that day and he sits down for long rests. Shooey took him for a short walk but no avail. I always feel he may have performed early in the morning. I lost my latch key this morning in the orchard but found it again after quarter of an hour.

I wonder if I shall see anything in the paper tomorrow. I told Shooey. She was really glad. I shan't tell any one else till tomorrow.

Good luck my dear
    Your loving Mother

    Alice M Rock.

Alice Rock
White House
Cranleigh
Surrey

18 June 1945

c/o Mrs James
The Chestnuts
Denbigh Road
Bletchley

My dearest Margaret

I hoped for a letter from you today, but the last post has been. It is a beautiful day - what June ought to be! We are all taking meals in the garden. Mr Crockett had 3 rabbits given him, he brought them home (2). I had one and they the other, a good change and larders full of meat. I took a little of mine for Mrs Luff and the boy. Tony had a wonderful dinner of the innards. I had some liver but they wouldn't touch it.

The strawberries are not very good, too much rain and humidity. We had a few each on Sunday, so many were mouldy - whole plants of it. Luff thinks the redcurrants ought to hold out till Saturday. He has mended most of nets if not I shall try my hand at jelly; but I feel nervous.

The whole family next door are going to London tomorrow. It looks as if it would be hot.

During last night we had a taste of the bad old days. An ammunition dump blew up. Windows smashed at Guildford.

The garden is looking lovely. We had a good dish of peas one day and we shall have another tomorrow. Tony had a good bath this morning. He lies about a lot but nose is cold.

I am having a chimney cleaned on Wednesday at 8am and our sitting room next Tuesday. Millie is coming on Wednesday to do the worst part. I expect we shall be in for a bit of a muddle for a day or two. I am having tea with Mrs Kennard tomorrow. So far the fruit is still with us!

I told your news next door and they were delighted. I don't know whether it will come off. She wants to go in July - she mentioned a date but Bushy said Nancy couldn't go that week.

Mrs Hopkinson has asked us to go there for a night when we go to Tidworth. That is as vague as all the rest. I don't suppose Shooey could stay again. She is searching all day for a house. Miss Taylor is going to share it and will be turned out of her present place long before Shooey finds a house. Norah has made a muddle about voting. She is not now on the register. This place has 3 candidates. Labour seems everywhere.

I hope the party was a great success and also the man's journey to London.

I think there is more work to do in the summer. Mostly in the garden and it never looks as if anything had ever been done.

My best love to you.

Your loving Mother Alice M Rock.

Barbara
Malcolm Club
H.Q. 124 Wing
R.A.F
B.L.A

25 June 1945

Miss M Rock
Box 111
Bletchley
Buck
England

Margaret dear,

Congratulations to you. This is only a very short note as I've just heard the good news from Rachel, so had to write a quick line.

Life is quite chaotic here. We get up at 8 (i.e. get to the Club at 8, and we get back at 10.30 at night - Eat sandwiches for lunch and dinner!! It has only been open for a week and so is still very unorganised. There are only 3 of us run it & one of them is new like me and just as useless!!

We are on an airfield at Lubeck and it will in time I suppose be fun - but at the moment rather chaotic.

Please forgive me more now, I will write properly later.

Lots of Love and I'm so glad about the M.B.E I haven't seen a paper since I left England.

Yours
Barbara

Miss Margaret Rock
M.B.E

22 October 1946

Central Chancery of
The Order of Knighthood
St. James's Palace
London
SW1

Madam,

I have the honour to send to you herewith the Warrant under The King's Sign Manual granting you the dignity of a Member of the Civil Division of the Most Excellent Order of the British Empire, and to inform you that the Insignia has been sent to you under separate registered cover.

Would you please be good enough to acknowledge the receipt of these on the attached form.

I have the honour to be, Madam,
Your obedient Servant,

Ivan De La Bere
Brigadier

Alice Maud Rock died 1951

Alice Rock Last Will & Testament

I Alice Maud Fanny Rock of 1 Taswell Road Southsea in the County of Hants Widow of Frank Ernest Rock MD hereby forsake all tesmentary instruments heretofore executive by me and declare this to be my last Will and testament. I appoint my daughter Margaret Alice Rock to be the sole Executrix of this Will but if she shall die before me or has not attained the age of twenty one years before my decease then I appoint my sister Floriel Rose Usborne and my brother Herbert Sydney Simmonds to the Executors of this Will.

I advise and bequeath all my estate and effects whatsoever and wheresoever is and to the use of my children Margaret Alice Rock and John Frank Rock or such of them as attains the age of twenty one years or (being my daughter) marries under that age and if more than one in equal shares and so that if either child dies in my lifetime leaving issue living at my death such child shall be deemed to have survived me and died in immediate after me.

I empower my Executrix or Executors to raise any part (not exceeding one money) of the presumptive share of either child of my estate and to apply by the same in addition to the whole or any part of the Income from such share for his or her maintenance or advancement or benefit.

I witness hereof I have herein set my hand this eighteenth day of February One Thousand nine hundred and eighteen.

Signed by the said Testatrix on her last Will in the presence of us who in her presence and Alice Maud Fanny Rock in the presence of each other have herewith subscribed our names as witnesses

[Alice left an estate worth £15,000 in 1951 to Margaret]

18 Fielder Avenue
Bull Farm
Mansfield
Notts

20 June 1952

Miss Margaret Rock
Westmead
The Avenue
Ickenham
Middlesex

Dear Miss Margaret,

Very sorry for being too long in a single letter of 15 June 1951.

Don't know whether your mother is still here or not, if so, I hope she is so comfortable as can be, in the circumstances.

You know Margaret one of the happiest times of my 4 1/2 years in the Army was at your mother's home in Cranleigh. Often long to go back there for a stay, but it would not be the same.

Don't remember you too much as we did not see much of you. Always remember arriving there I thought the maid was the daughter of the house, your mother treated her servant that well, as that was the impression received by a total stranger.

How well she treated us, one occasion I had a very bad cold, and your mother said if I did not report sick she would tell the C.O. as you no doubt know know he was killed with Froggatt, and the adjutant, leaving me the only survivor.

I was lay in hospital recovering from my wounds when I received through the press the news of your dear brother, this hurt, very much as I thought right away of our very great friend, your mother.

This letter is very sad I am afraid, we should not live in the past, but we cannot help thinking sometimes of the ones we loved and respected so much.

Well how is your uncle these days, whom visited Cranleigh, your father's brother, I understand your mother to say. He was on the same shift as father.

You still work in the Foreign Office I see, plenty of trouble there nowadays, I suppose nothing but trouble. But your mother had plenty of trouble, and stood up to it, so we must do the same.

Do you ever get up to this part of the country, or does your work keep you static?

Keep smiling
        yours sincerely

        Leonard Dickinson

CHAPTER SEVEN

Retiring in Worcetershire

On 7 July 1963 Margaret retired from her life at GCHQ. She was 60 years old. Aided by a pension and private income Margaret was able to live comfortably, but frugally with her companion Norah Sheward.

Her income also allowed Margaret to continue with her love for travel. Norah's papers are full of the postcards she collected, some of which are from Margaret briefly describing her travels. Despite the bond of friendship, Margaret continued to be an independent spirit, as she had been when John was alive.

Norah was rather a domineering and bossy woman, a contrast to the quiet self assurance of Margaret, who did not engage in confrontation.

Margaret purchased a plot of land in the neighbouring parish of Bredon's Norton and built a bungalow for her and Norah to spend their old age.

Retirement buzzed along quietly this rural, picturesque Worcestershire as they tended their lush, colourful cottage garden. They also enjoyed music and, in their seventies, they enjoyed the more active pursuit of taking a boat into the river and gathering reeds for basket making.

Margaret was well into her seventies before the first story about code breaking at Bletchley Park hit the headlines. Despite a reticence borne from years of silence, Margaret began to share snippets about her time at Bletchley Park.

She never spoke openly about the work, especially as her work at GCHQ was still covered by the Official Secret Act.

Her relative Charles recalls that despite the passing years, she held Dilly Knox still in high regard. She always held the memory of Dilly and her time at Bletchley close to her heart. She also never lost her sense of awe for her adventurous and charismatic brother,John.

Margaret talked about her love for numbers but she never did share the full extent of her personal experiences during the war. Her own account of events are immortalised in the technical history she wrote along with other codebreakers. The official history of the Abwehr codebreaking operation was referred to as 'Batey, Batey, Rock and Twinn,' after its authors. The document, covering the codebreaking techniques used in great detail was considered so sensitive that it is has only been released into the public domain in recent years. The last surviving author, Mavis Batey was given a copy during a ceremony in September 2011.

Mavis and Margaret kept in touch, with Margaret joining Batey family on holiday. They welcomed Margaret into the family asking her to be Godmother to their daughter, Elizabeth. Margaret wrote to Elizabeth on the 11 July 1983 about meeting her Bletchley Park friends at her birthday celebration.

'We had a lovely party at Jean Perrin's with your parents yesterday We sat for hours after lunch just talking, it was so pleasant.'

The following month Margaret collapsed at the doctor's surgery, where she had gone for the check up required for keeping her driving licence. She was taken to Ronkswood Hospital, Worcester where she died on 26 August 1983.

Margaret has a small square memorial stone in the church yard at Bredon's Norton church. It is small and discreet, just like the woman it for.

Margaret Rock August 1982

In the High Court of Justice
The Probate Registry of Wales

BE IT KNOWN that **MARGARET ALICE ROCK** of Middle Croft, Bredons Norton in the County of Hereford and Worcester died on the **25th day of August 1983** domiciled in England and Wales

AND FURTHER IT BE KNOWN that at the date hereunder written the last Will and Testament

(a copy whereof is hereunto annexed) of the said deceased was proved and registered in the

Probate Registry of Wales of the High Court of Justice

and Administration of the all the estate which by law devolves to and vests in the personal representative of the said deceased was granted by the aforesaid Court to CHARLES FRANCIS FOSTER of and JOHN OLIVER DIXON and ROBERT GEORGE OTTER the executors named in the said Will

It is hereby certified that it appears from the information supplied on the application for the grant that the gross value of the said estate in the United Kingdom

I hereby certify that from the information supplied for the grant that the gross value of the said Estate in Great Britain amounts to £212979.02 and that the net value of such estate amounts to £212381.72

Dated 10th day of November 1983

JL Allen
Probate Officer

Extracted by Moore Brown & Dixon 69/70 High Street Tewkesbury, Glos

HOW TO ACCESS EXCLUSIVE MATERIAL

www.dearcodebreaker.com

To access the exclusive material only available to purchasers of this book, go to www.dearcodebreaker.com and enter the following code in the password box.

You do not need give any personal details to access the website. Just use the code shown below and following the instructions online:

15BP#Cr-fT83

Please feel free to sign up to receive the Dear CodeBreaker newsletter to receive notification when new material posted to the website. Your details will never be shared and you will only receive information about Dear CodeBreaker. You can unsubscribe at any time.

Finally, please do not give away the code for free. At least 20% of the profit from this book will be donated between the Bletchley Park Trust, Buckinghamshire and the Airborne Assault Museum, Duxford so every book sale counts.

Thank you for purchasing and reading this book. You can find out more about me, Kerry Howard, and my research on my primary website
www.bletchleyparkresearch.co.uk

BIBLIOGRAPHY

Chapter 1 - Early Years 1903 - 1916

Frank Ernest Rock's Royal Navy Service Record, The National Archives (TNA) ADM 196/10/504

Untitled Newspaper Article, 10 February 1917 (Margaret's papers) www.ancestry.co.uk

Chapter Two- Getting Ahead in Education 1917 - 1925

Margaret's University Records - Bedford College, Royal Holloway Archives, University of London BC.AR.300.1391

Portsmouth High School 1882 - 1957, M.E. Howell, Girls' Public Day School Trust & Grovsenor Press, circa 1957

A History of Bedford College for Women 1949-1937, by Margaret Tuke, Oxford University Press 1939

Chapter Three Adventurous Adults 1926 - 1938

John Frank Rock's Army Service Record, MOD Personnel Service

Saar Territory - www.wikipedia.com

Chapter Four - The Road to France 1939 - 1940

War in France & Flanders, Major L.F. Ellis, Naval & Military Press 2009

The Maginot Line, Rudolph Chelminski, Smithsonian Article 1997

Chapter Five - Bletchley Park & RAF Ringway 1940 - 1945

Action This Day , Michael Smith & Ralph Erskine, Bantam Press, 2001

Dilly - The Man Who Broke Enigmas by Mavis Batey, Biteback Publishing 2010

The Secrets of Station X - How the Bletchley Park Codebreakers Helped Win the War, Michael Smith, Biteback Publishing, 2011

Page Dilly's letter to ISK January 1943 TNA HW25/12

Denniston's Memo to Menzies, TNA HW14/22

Churchill's Spearhead - The Development of Britain's Airborne Forces during the Second World War, John Greenacre, Pen & Sword Aviation, 2010

The Guinea-Pigs - Britains First Partroop Raid, Raymond Foxall, Robert Hale Ltd, 1983

The Wooden Sword, Lawrence Wright, Elek Books Ltd, 1967

Chapter Six - Cold War Codebeaking at GCHQ 1946 - 1963

GCHQ - Richard Aldrich, Harper Press 2010

Made in the USA
Charleston, SC
14 August 2013